Living Design

Living Design

the Daoist way of building

C. Thomas Mitchell
and
Jiangmei Wu

McGraw-Hill

New York   San Francisco   Washington, DC   Auckland   Bogotá
Caracas   Lisbon   London   Madrid   Mexico City   Milan
Montreal   New Delhi   San Juan   Singapore
Sydney   Tokyo   Toronto

McGraw-Hill

A Division of The McGraw·Hill Companies

Permissions

From THE TAO OF PHYSICS by Fritjof Capra. © 1973, 1983, 1991. Reprinted by arrangement with Shambhala Publications, Inc., Boston.

From BECOME WHAT YOU ARE by Alan Watts. © 1995 by Mark Watts. Reprinted by arrangement with Shambhala Publications, Inc., Boston.

From THE TAO TEH CHING by Lao Tzu, translated by John C. H. Wu. © 1961 by St. John's University Press, New York. Reprinted by arrangement with Shambhala Publications, Inc., Boston.

From FENG SHUI: THE CHINESE ART OF PLACEMENT by Sarah Rossbach. Copyright © 1983 by Sarah Rossbach. Used by permission of Dutton Signet, a division of Penguin Books USA Inc.

"The Chinese Geomancer", from WHAT AM I DOING HERE? by Bruce Chatwin. Copyright © 1989 by the Estate of Bruce Chatwin. Used by permission of Viking Penguin, a division of Penguin Books USA Inc.

1 2 3 4 5 6 7 8 9 0 KGP/KGP 9 0 3 2 1 0 9 8
ISBN 0-07-042975-8

This book is printed on acid-free paper

Credits
The sponsoring editor for this book was Wendy Lochner, the editing supervisor was Peggy Lamb, and the production supervisor was Sherri Souffrance. It was designed and set in Monotype Dante and Monotype Gill by Claire Mitchell.

Printed and bound by Quebecor/Kingsport Press.

Library of Congress Cataloging-in-Publication Data

Mitchell, C. Thomas.
    Living design : the Daoist way building / C. Thomas Mitchell and Jiangmei Wu.
    p.   cm.
    Includes bibliographical references and indes.
    ISBN 0-07-042975-8
    1. Architectural design. 2. Architecture—Human factors.
3. Taoism. I. Wu, Jiangmei. II. Title.
NA2750.M55   1998
720'.108—dc21
                                          97-39997
                                             CIP

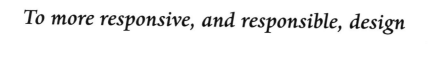

To more responsive, and responsible, design

Contents

Preface

Over the course of the past few decades interest in Eastern philosophy and thought, and the ways in which they can influence how we do things in the West, has grown markedly. There have been books on Zen and the art of, among other things, rhetoric, the Internet, writing, teaching, painting, and archery, as well as ones on Dao and philosophy, work, inner peace, negotiation, physics, Pooh, psychology, and time. No matter how tenuous the connection between the Eastern philosophies and the Western activities that they are conjoined with, the premise of each of these books is that there is a wisdom present in the traditions of the East that is missing in present-day Western society—a wisdom that, it is hoped, can be tapped in order to make the activities we engage in more meaningful.

This book is the product of a collaboration exploring the relevance and applicability of Eastern philosophical ideas to design and architecture in the West. The partnership of myself and Jiangmei Wu occurred by chance, but was fortuitous. At the time we met, I was completing my first book, *Redefining designing: From form to experience,* in which I set out the shortcomings of recent trends in Western architecture and design and argued for a new, more user responsive approach to designing. Mei, having completed an undergraduate degree in architecture in China, was pursuing a master's degree in interior design because it was her intention to adapt her skills in order to practice architecture and design in the United States. I'm afraid I ruined things for her somewhat by my insistence that the processes of Western design are fundamentally flawed and by suggesting that a more worthwhile course for her might be to undertake a project demonstrating the interrelationship of philosophy and form that is central to traditional Chinese architecture. This book is based on Mei's research project exploring this topic, but the material has been totally recast in order to demonstrate its relevance to those in the West.

There have been a number of books written that present the formal characteristics of Chinese towns, buildings, and gardens, as well as numerous ones on Chinese philosophy and thought. In addition, there has been a proliferation of books of late on Feng Shui, the Chinese art of placement, as applied to all scales of designing. This book is different from those presently available. Though traditional Chinese architecture is discussed throughout, this is not a volume devoted to architectural history per se. Instead of considering the building as an object, we explore the role of architecture in people's lives and illustrate how it serves as a reflection of their belief system.

Unlike many of the books written on Feng Shui, it is *not* our contention that forms and philosophies from the East should be directly imported into Western design. Nor do we believe, as some other authors suggest, that there is a "magical" power behind the forms that Eastern techniques such as Feng Shui give rise to. Instead, we recognize in such approaches an attention to aspects of design experience that should be addressed in every culture but are often neglected in the West. The intention of this book is to present the essential nature of Eastern thought, to demonstrate how it influences built form, and, most importantly in this context, to set out its relevance to present and emerging trends in Western design.

It is our firm belief that there are at present endemic problems in Western design. Though symptoms—such as hard-to-use, dangerous products or alienating buildings filled with carcinogenic materials—are frequently discussed, there is great reluctance to admit that the system that gives rise to these is itself to blame. Instead, there are ongoing attempts to "paper over the cracks" and pretend that such problems are anomalies. Eastern philosophy provides a broader, less expedient, perspective. Lao Tzu [Laozi], in the *Tao Teh Ching* [Dao De Jing], wrote:

> To realize that our knowledge is ignorance,
> This is a noble insight.
> To regard our ignorance as knowledge,
> This is mental sickness.
>
> Only when we are sick of our sickness
> Shall we cease to be sick.
> The Sage is not sick, being sick of sickness;
> This is the secret of health.[1]

This poem has direct relevance to the current state of designing. Much of what we regard as "good design" is, itself, merely a component of a broader, more pervasive, problem. It is not the aim of this book, however, to explore the sickness and ignorance that underpin Western design in detail. The focus, instead, will be on the ways in which Eastern philosophy can be applied in the West in order to make designs that are truly meaningful and healthy.

In particular, we hope that what is in these pages will help those who have been uncomfortable or unsatisfied by their interactions with objects or environments to understand the reasons for their dissatisfaction and to articulate responses to it. We also hope that designers from all disciplines will find the book to be of use and that the broad perspective provided by Daoist thought serves to inspire more humane and responsive design work. For those who have an interest in emerging trends such as Feng Shui and Green Design, we have attempted to assess their role and significance in the evolving design debate. Through careful consideration of the qualities that characterize traditional Chinese architecture—such as harmony at all scales of designing, integration with nature, and strong cultural and spritual connections—we can rediscover much that has been lost in recent years in the West.

Tom Mitchell
(mitchelc@indiana.edu)
Yellowwood Forest, Indiana
Spring 1998

Acknowledgments

In my writing on design, I have worked in what John Chris Jones would term a "contextual" manner, identifying the worthwhile and innovative thoughts of others and packaging them in what I hope is an accessible manner. Because of this approach, my writing is less an individual quest than a record of collaborative activity. Though books appear at intervals, the research process goes on continually. A number of people support and encourage me in this process providing timely advice and criticism. The most notable of these people is John Chris Jones, who has outlined an intriguing and enlivening future for design that too few people have recognized and explored. John Chris has been central to my thinking and writing since I was an undergraduate; over the past 16 years he has helped me in innumerable ways. Also essential to me have been the insights of Andy King, a constant companion via e-mail for a number of years, who provides perspective on all of my work through his often extensive, and always thoughtful and witty, comments.

The reference librarians at Indiana University have cheerfully taken a personal interest in my work, going well beyond their job descriptions to keep my projects moving. Jeff Graf in particular takes on the burden of much of my research so that I am freed up for writing; he also painstakingly reviewed all of the bibliographical references cited in this book to ensure their accuracy. Carol LeBras and Erika Dowell of the Fine Arts Library have also provided indispensable help. I have been extremely lucky, as well, to have had a range of outstanding graduate students. Steve Awoniyi in particular has been an excellent sounding board for me as I conduct my research and write, providing very helpful suggestions on an ongoing basis. Thanks too to the kind and patient staff at the Bakehouse, on the square in Bloomington, where most of this book was written and edited.

A number of people played essential roles in the conception and realization of this book. Wendy Lochner of McGraw-Hill, who commissioned the book, is the very model of what an acquisitions editor should be. She is genuinely interested in advancing the state of design thinking. Thanks too to Peggy Lamb, McGraw-Hill's Editing Manager, and to Marci Nugent for her careful copy editing. Claire Mitchell has done an outstanding job in designing the book, making clear the essential relationship between images and text.

Special thanks go to those who helped me assemble the book's art package, including: Geoffrey Taylor, of the Indiana University Architects' Office; James and Chris Wines of SITE, Inc.; Charles Rosenblum of William McDonough + Partners; Bernard Tschumi of Columbia University; Lucien Kroll of Atelier Lucien Kroll, Brussels; Melanie Maxwell of the Columbus (Indiana) Area Visitors Center; Delle Willett of the Missouri Botanical Gardens; Terry Foo of the Hongkong and Shanghai Banking Corporation; Julie Rutherford of Historical New Harmony (Indiana); and Darnell Lautt of the Wexner Center for the Arts. Thanks too are due to the kind permissions editors at a variety of publishers and publications for their permission to reprint text in this volume. Also critical was David Keenan, of Indiana University's East Asian Summer Language Institute, who reviewed several drafts of the manuscript and provided advice on the use of the Pinyin system of romanization and on a range of other technical issues concerning the book's subject matter. Thanks, too, are due to Thomas Lee, Indiana University's East Asian subject area librarian who helped clear up some murky issues for me. Without the help of these people this book could not have been written.

In the broader context, I depend on the support, insights, and tolerance of my wife Claire for whom this whole process has become a way of life. We are both indebted to our Buddhist friends and to our teachers for their kind instruction in the dharma. My heartfelt thanks, in particular, go to my spiritual guide Geshe-La.

C.T.M.

I would like to express my appreciation to my master's thesis committee members: Tom Mitchell, Kate Rowold, and Sue Tuohy. Sue carefully reviewed the drafts of my text and made numerous very helpful suggestions. I am also very grateful for Kate's ongoing support throughout the process, as well. The librarians of the Fine Arts Library of Indiana University, B. J. Irvine and Lara Ingaman, have been essential to me in providing the sometimes obscure resources I've needed to complete this work. To conclude, I want to thank my dear friend Karl Corts for his moral and spiritual support.

J.W.

Authors' Note

In this book we have used the "Pinyin" system of romanization that was officially adopted by the People's Republic of China in 1958. Some words that may be familiar to readers in the previously common Wade-Giles system will, therefore, be different. For example "Ch'i" becomes "Qi," "Tao" becomes "Dao," and *I Ching* becomes *Yi Jing*. Where English editions of Chinese books using the Wade-Giles system are cited, their Pinyin titles are given in brackets. Where a word transcribed using the Wade-Giles system appears in an English language book (for example, *The Tao of Physics*), no Pinyin equivalent is given.

Unless otherwise indicated, all of the visual material presented in this book is by Jiangmei Wu. The models were photographed by Mark Simons, and the photographs were digitally enhanced by Jiangmei Wu. Unless otherwise indicated, all images in this book are oriented to the north.

1

Introduction

Reassessing Western design

Design and architecture have been in a state of continuous crisis since the failure of modernism began to be acknowledged in the 1960s. In the wake of this there have been numerous attempts to make designing more responsive to users, but these reactions, such as postmodernism, can now be seen to be little more than superficial changes of fashion that do not address the fundamental problems at the core of the crisis.[1] Though there are many definitions that illustrate the basis of these problems, perhaps the best, and most influential, example comes from the late architectural historian Sir Nikolaus Pevsner, who wrote:

> A bicycle shed is a building; Lincoln Cathedral is a piece of architecture. Nearly everything that encloses space on a scale sufficient for a human being to move in is a building; the term architecture applies only to buildings designed with a view to aesthetic appeal.[2]

As this quote indicates, the focus of architectural activity has not been on producing "bicycle sheds," which might ideally fulfill their purposes.[3] Instead the energies of architects and designers have been siphoned off into the pursuit of "aesthetic appeal," often at the expense of a meaningful consideration of the many different needs that design must address if it is to suit

Mies van der Rohe. Apartment housing, oblique view of facade from Bruckmannweg, Weissenhofsiedlung, Stuttgart, Germany, 1927. *(Photo: C. Thomas Mitchell, taken in 1982)*

Victor Bourgeois. House facade, view from Friedrich Ebert Strasse, Weissenhofsiedlung, Stuttgart, Germany, 1927. *(Photo: C. Thomas Mitchell, taken in 1982)*

J. J. P. Oud. Rowhousing, oblique view from Pankokweg, Weissenhofsiedlung, Stuttgart, Germany, 1927. *(Photo: C. Thomas Mitchell, taken in 1982)*

the needs of those who interact with it. Architecture, in Pevsner's view, can be judged on its merits as visual art, without reference to the purpose it is to serve.

Though the separation of aesthetics from function has had very negative consequences for design, there is, in fact, a more serious problem with Pevsner's contention. Lincoln Cathedral is a successful and imposing building owing to the fact that its form is governed, in large part, by the need to rely on and embed a well-understood belief system in its design. Further, the form of the cathedral was determined to a profound degree by its method of construction — it was built according to time-honored conventions by Master Builders.

Despite all of this, however, it is common for architectural historians to appropriate whole areas of building activity for architecture, when in fact aesthetics, in the sense Pevsner uses the term, played a very small role in determining the appearance of Lincoln Cathedral, or any other religious building of its time. Jan Swafford addressed this point, noting, "When a Western visitor to the East once complimented his host country's arts, a priest replied, 'We don't have any arts. We just do everything the best we can.'"[4]

It is the sense of the interconnectedness of physical forms, and the belief systems that give rise to them, that is often missing from writing on architecture. Instead, a fictional history is presented that imputes our present view of the architect as an individualistic genius onto buildings that were actually the product of collaborative efforts based on shared belief systems. So, ironically, few of the historic buildings that architects study, sketch, and photograph were produced by a process even resembling that which is now used in architecture, in which objects are planned via drawing (on paper or computer) in isolation from users and constructed by armies of workers who can do nothing to personally influence the building's appearance. This process is quite different from that employed by the artisans of the Middle Ages, and it leads to quite different outcomes.

With the advent of modernism, architects found themselves unencumbered by constraints such as the height limitations imposed by load-bearing walls, and they no longer had to possess a detailed understanding of the construction processes by which their buildings were built. So what in fact happened when architects became free to plan whatever they liked in the abstract, without reference to commonly held belief systems?

The result, as has been widely documented,[5] was a profound alienation of the public from architecture.

When one now views the monuments of modernism, such as Le Corbusier's Villa Savoye in France or the buildings in the Weissenhof Colony in Stuttgart, it isn't just that the structures are physically crumbling that makes them appear lifeless. And they don't appear dead simply because the modernist ideas on which they were based have proven faulty. Rather, they are profoundly depressing because they provide tangible evidence of what results from the belief that architecture can be produced and judged in isolation from the context in which it is placed. As such, they are emblematic of the wider crisis facing design.

Though this separation of theory and context is most obvious with modernism, it is also true of more recent movements. Richard Meier's Atheneum in New Harmony, Indiana, designed in the late-modern style, stands as an object lesson in the extension of Le Corbusier's principles of geometry, and the inability of the building materials industry to approach that perfection. Postmodernism, early critics charged, would be okay until the paint faded. With Charles Moore's Piazza d'Italia in New Orleans, one of the most photographed examples of postmodernism, this is certainly the case. Though not yet 20 years old, it has become a folly, in ruins well before its time. This "stage set" quality is also characteristic of other icons of postmodern architecture, such as Venturi and Rauch's Fire Station No. 4 in Columbus, Indiana. It hardly seems necessary

Richard Meier and Associates. The Atheneum/Visitor's Center, interior view, New Harmony, Indiana, 1979. *(Photo courtesy of University of Southern Indiana/Historic New Harmony)*

Richard Meier and Associates. The Atheneum/Visitor's Center, exterior view, New Harmony, Indiana, 1979. *(Photo courtesy of University of Southern Indiana/ Historic New Harmony)*

Venturi and Rauch. Fire Station
No. 4, exterior view, Columbus,
Indiana, 1967. *(Photo courtesy
Columbus Area Visitors Center)*

to explore the disjunction between theory and reality in deconstructive architecture, as that is the very aim of the movement. An excerpt from an interview with a leading architect of the movement, Peter Eisenman, leaves little doubt about the intention of his work. Architectural historian Charles Jencks asked, "So your definition of Modernism as alienation is first of all, as you have already admitted, only really possible outside of architecture, it isn't true of architecture." To which Eisenman replied:

> It has not been true of architecture, but I think it should be. I think it's more difficult in architecture because, as I have said on many occasions, architecture is so rooted in presence and in seeing itself as shelter and institution, house and home. It is the guardian of reality. It is the last bastion of location. I think this is the real problem. Architecture represses dislocation because of the paradoxical position it maintains. You don't have that problem with theology or philosophy or science.[6]

Eisenman is a problematic figure in the architectural firmament because he actually says what is implicit, if unacknowledged, in the work of many other major architects. Though it probably is *not* true that most architects *seek* to make their work alienating, as Eisenman assures us he does with his own, given the philosophy on which their work is based, and the methods used in its production, "dislocation" (to use Eisenman's term) is the natural result.

The alienation of the public from architecture results directly from the view that buildings are art objects that need conform only to the architect's criteria of success. Not only architecture but the whole of Western thinking is based on such an "object-oriented" view in which too much attention is paid to the "subject" and too little to the "context." This relationship was addressed by the late philosopher Alan Watts who wrote:

> For before we can truly appreciate the changing individuality of things we must, in a certain sense, realize their unreality. That is to say, one must understand that not only oneself, but all other things in the universe are meaningless and dead when considered by themselves, as permanent, isolated, self-sufficient entities.[7]

So much of our built environment in the West is perceived to be meaningless and dead as a result of this object-oriented focus of architecture and design. Though this leads to problems with conventional design, the challenge faced by the design professions is further intensified as the nature of design tasks undergoes rapid transformation. Alongside architecture and product design for which, in the short term at least, an object-oriented approach was an expedient, there is now a range of design tasks, such as the design of computer operating systems, that have no physical presence.[8] For designers trained in the planning of form through drawings, this transition to intangible, process-based designing can be a difficult one. These tasks require a whole range of new skills and sensitivities.

The prevalence of unsolved problems with tangible designs, such as architecture and product design, and the emergence of new, intangible design tasks highlight the need for a new approach to design. The primary focus of such a design should not be on form but on the many layers of connections—cultural, social, and psychological—through which people interact with design. It is not enough just to modify our existing processes; rather new ones based on a more comprehensive view of the role and importance of design must be developed.

Eisenman/Trott Architects, Inc. New York. Partners-in-Charge: Peter Eisenman, Richard Trott, Wexner Center for the Arts, Columbus, Ohio, 1989. View of the Wexner Center from the southeast. (Photo: Kevin Fitzsimons/Wexner Center for the Arts, The Ohio State University)

Eisenman/Trott Architects, Inc. New York. Partners-in-Charge: Peter Eisenman, Richard Trott, Wexner Center for the Arts, Columbus, Ohio, 1989. View of grand staircase from lower lobby with upper lobby in background. (Photo: Kevin Fitzsimons/Wexner Center for the Arts, The Ohio State University)

Eastern and Western thought

Eastern thought and philosophy present an alternative way of viewing the world, one that has particular relevance as we seek to transcend the limitations imposed by the object orientation in design. The basis of the distinction between Eastern and Western views is succinctly summed up in the context of language by Alan Watts. He noted:

> In English the differences between things and actions are clearly, if not always logically, distinguished, but a great number of Chinese words do duty for both nouns and verbs— so that one who thinks in Chinese has little difficulty in seeing that objects are also events, that our world is a collection of processes rather than entities.[9]

It is this transition from viewing the world as a collection of things, to a belief in interconnected processes, that is critical. For architects and designers it is particularly important to shift our attention from nouns to verbs — addressing not just the objects that occupy the world but, more importantly, the processes through which they interrelate and the ways in which people interact with them over time.

As noted earlier, however, the philosophy of Western design is simply a reflection of the broader culture of which it is a part. Though they are rarely examined, the cultural assumptions on which the object orientation are based are worthy of investigation. Alan Watts was one of the first to compare the very different views of the world held by those in the East and West. He pointed out:

> The whole of Western thought is profoundly influenced through and through by the idea that all things—all events, all people, all mountains, all stars, all flowers, all grasshoppers, all worms—are artifacts; they have been made. It is therefore natural for a Western child to say to its mother, "How was I made?" On the other hand, that would be quite an unnatural question for a Chinese child, because the Chinese do not think of nature as something that was made. Instead they look upon it as something that grows, and the two processes are quite different. When you make something you put it together: you assemble parts, or you

carve an image out of wood or stone, working from the
outside to the inside. However, when you watch something
grow, it works in an entirely different way. It does not
assemble its parts. It expands from within and gradually com-
plicates itself, expanding outwards, like a bud blossoming or
a seed turning into a plant.[10]

This distinction between making and growing is fundamental. Western architecture and design are devoted to making (or
rather planning for others to make), as opposed to setting into
motion a process of growth through which a building or product will evolve and adapt as circumstances change. This process
of evolution happens to all physical artifacts in context; the
question is whether they resist this change or accommodate it
gracefully.[11] One need only compare a highrise towerblock to
an English farmhouse to appreciate the degree to which architecture can inhibit or support the process of growth and
adaptation in use.

There are a range of cultural and personal implications of
the object orientation as well. As Watts notes:

We become clock-dominated, and the abstract system takes
over from the physical, organic situation. As a result, we have
run into a cultural situation where we have confused the
symbol with the physical reality, the money with the wealth,
the menu with the dinner, and as a result we are starving
from eating menus.[12]

In architecture and design, just this situation has transpired.
An abstract system of aesthetics has taken over from the
organic reality of building, to the extent that there is now a
number of very well regarded architects who have constructed
few if any buildings.[13] Instead, they have become noteworthy
through their drawings and models. These artifacts demonstrate
the way in which they manipulate the visual, aesthetic codes
valued by architects and designers and are a clear reflection of
the true interests of the profession. We have, as Watts points
out, "confused the symbol with the physical reality," but the
"menus" that architects and designers offer up for our
consumption are, on the whole, most unfulfilling.

In order to make Western architecture and design more
healthy, the basic premises on which it is based must be chal-
lenged. The focus on individual objects made in isolation must

be abandoned in favor of a view in which all elements of designing, and their impacts, are considered. We must abandon the process through which designs are conceived on a drawing board in a studio and viewed as inviolable solutions. Such designs are destined to be failures in a world of constant change. Instead, the role of a designer should be to set in motion a process of growth, creating designs that can develop over time. It is here that Eastern philosophy—with its emphasis on growing, not making; on process, rather than product; and on connection, instead of separation—can be so instructive to us in the West.

The qualities of living design

A number of trends aimed at making Western design more healthy are now emerging. Perhaps the most notable, and publicized, of these approaches is *Green Design*.[14] Advocates of this approach consider the longer-term consequences of design decisions, for people individually and collectively, and for the ecosystem as a whole.

Another area that is being recognized on a culture-wide basis is the need for a stronger spiritual foundation for our actions. This is a particularly poignant issue in design, for many of the great buildings of the past that are admired were constructed not just to fulfill pragmatic, temporal aims but instead were seen as symbols of, or offerings to, the gods. A number of architects are now exploring the use of a spiritual focus as the basis for their work, rather than confining themselves to functional considerations.[15]

Related to the loss of spirituality is a concern with the lack of meaning or, to put it less politely, the banality of much recent design. Several reactions have developed in response to this. In architecture, for example, postmodernists have used symbolism from the past or from pop culture in an attempt to infuse their work with meaning.[16] In product design a similar trend has manifested itself. Concerned by the anonymity of so many designs, interpretive designers use metaphors to make the purpose of objects, and the processes by which they are to be used, clear.[17]

An additional dimension is beginning to be considered as well—the nature of the experience and use of a design over time. *Narrative architects,* for example, focus explicitly in their work on the quality of experience that people will have in the spaces that they design.[18] Others have considered the experience of design by, for example, looking at the use of office spaces over time,[19] the ways buildings change during their lives,[20] and the perceptions that different types of environments give rise to.[21]

In fact, of course, none of these areas—ecological responsiveness, the quest for higher meaning, or the consideration of the use and experience of design over time—can be separated. These concerns are present to a greater or lesser extent in all successful design work. With the fragmentation of design into different subdisciplines—and the division of labor that keeps users, designers (planners), and makers separate—it is, however, very difficult to ensure that all of these considerations are adequately accounted for. Not surprisingly, they very rarely are.

In contrast, Chinese architecture and design have traditionally been fully integrated with the country's culture and belief systems. The principles on which it has been based include:

1. Harmony at all scales of design
2. Integration with nature
3. Strong cultural connections
4. The importance of shared understanding of environmental meaning
5. An emphasis on the process of experiencing design, not on form alone
6. A focus on placemaking, not space planning

Though none of the forms of Chinese architecture should be directly imported to the West, these central concepts can be adapted by Western designers to make their work more responsive, meaningful, and experientially rich.

In the chapters that follow, the basic principles of Chinese philosophy, with an emphasis on Daoism, will be set out. Specific attention will be given to the way in which Daoist thought underpins the form of Chinese towns, buildings, and gardens. The practice of Feng Shui, which is perhaps the best-known means through which Eastern ideas are integrated into design, will also be critically examined.

The presence of Daoist concepts in built form at different design scales — town planning, religious structures, houses, and gardens — will then be explored in detail. For each different design task, such as choosing a town's site, the philosophy governing design decision making will be presented, along with a prototypical design embodying the principles, and a series of historic examples, showing how adaptations have been made to suit different contexts, will also be cited. In every case numerous illustrations will be provided to help clarify the presence of the Daoist principles in the design.

Though the study of Daoist ideas and traditional Chinese architecture is interesting in and of itself, the greatest benefit can be derived from this work by adapting these concepts for use by Western designers. The relationship of Daoist thinking to emerging design trends—such as Green Design and spiritually, symbolically, and narratively based architecture and design —and the use and experience of design over time will all be explored.

As noted earlier, however, this is not a "how-to" book. Instead, the intention is to provide alternative ways of thinking about design—approaches that are broader, deeper, and more integrated than those presently employed by the design professions. Daoist philosophy, and its application to design at all scales, shows clearly the way through which we can escape the moribund legacy of recent design and embrace a new, living philosophy of architecture and design.

2

Daoist principles

Daoist philosophy in context

Though Eastern thought is often discussed, as it has been thus far in this book, as if it constituted a single approach, there are in fact many different, and sometimes contradictory, philosophies in the East. In the belief system that underpinned traditional Chinese architecture, for example, there were three main forces: Buddhism, Confucianism, and Daoism. Buddhism is primarily focused on the mind, and its adherents' primary concern is the achievement of enlightenment, or release from ordinary existence. Confucianism is principally concerned with rules of order in society, whereas Daoists seek to understand, and merge with, the nature of things as they are. In *The Tao of Physics* Fritjof Capra noted of the relationship of Confucianism to Daoism:

> Confucianism was the philosophy of social organization, of common sense and practical knowledge. It provided Chinese society with a system of education and with strict conventions of social etiquette. One of its main purposes was to form an ethical basis for the traditional Chinese family system with its complex structure and its rituals of ancestor worship. Taoism [Daoism], on the other hand, was concerned primarily with the observation of nature and the discovery of its Way, or *Tao* [Dao]. Human happiness, according to the Taoists [Daoists], is achieved when men

follow the natural order, acting spontaneously and trusting their intuitive knowledge.[1]

It is this emphasis in Daoist thought on the grounding of action in the natural order that is so important for those of us in the West. Though, as has just been pointed out, it is impossible to truly disentangle these strands of thought from one another, the focus of our examination in this book will be on Daoism and its influence on built form. In order to explore Daoist ideas, however, it is first necessary to develop at least a cursory understanding of the Daoists' view of the universe.

According to Daoist beliefs, the universe began with the infinite—Wuji—the invisible vital force which was the very essence of its beings. Once it acquired form, it became the absolute—Taiji—the beginning of the physical universe that couldn't be known through our senses. The absolute, Taiji, breathed Qi, and created two forces, the Yin and the Yang, or negative and positive forces. Things thus created could either be Yin or Yang dominated. Yin, for example, dominated the earth, all that was negative, female, dark, wet, soft, cold, dead, or still. Yang, on the other hand, dominated heaven and all that was positive, male, light, fiery, hard, warm, living, and moving. Yin and Yang permeated the whole of the universe whose very life and breath was Qi.

The Yin and Yang forces were not considered to be things in and of themselves. Most things in the universe, however, were the final products of the interaction of these forces. The immediate products of Yin and Yang interaction were the Five Elements: metal, wood, water, fire, and earth. The Five Elements were the simplest forms of physical existence and were the essence of the physical universe that we human beings recognize through the five senses. Through various means the Five Elements in turn created the more complicated things such as trees and clouds—so, for example, a tree had "wood virtue" and a cloud had "water virtue." Everything in the universe, including human beings, had one of these five virtues.

The Five Elements produced and destroyed each other successively. In the productive process, wood caught fire and changed into ashes, the ashes went back to the earth which, after many years, became metal. The metal could then be melted into a liquid, such as water, to breed thousands of trees and begin the whole process again. In the destructive process, the earth made clear water turbid, the water put out fire, which could itself melt metal, and sharp metal could cut wood. Wood got its nutrition from the earth, and so the process continued.[2] Through the mutually productive and destructive sequence of the Five Elements, the "ten thousand things," which were believed to compose the universe, each acquired one of the five virtues. The Five Elements were also called "Xing," which literally meant the "Five Moving Agents."

The moving circle of the Five Elements could be arranged in another way with the earth element at the center. In this arrangement the Five Elements were always associated with five colors, four seasons, and the symbolic animals of each of the four quarters. Blue-green, for example, was associated with the warm spring, it was the color of the spring wood sprouts, and it accompanied the dragon of the east. Red was associated with the hot summer, it was the color of fire, and it was linked to the phoenix of the south. White was associated with the autumn, it was the color of metal, and it accompanied the tiger of the west. Black corresponded to winter, it was the color of the water abyss, which was associated with the sign of the turtle in the north. Yellow referred to the earth, it was the color of the earth, and it was placed at the center.[3]

Though the universe was thought to be eternal, so was change. Change, however, did not occur in a random way; it followed a definite pattern as set out in the "Eight Trigrams." The two opposing forces of Yin and Yang interacted to produce each of the Eight Trigrams. These consisted of three Yin or Yang lines, with Yin symbolized by broken lines and Yang symbolized by unbroken lines. The combination of three lines of either Yin or Yang placed one above the other produced the eight possible Trigrams. Further, these Eight Trigrams were paired with one another to form an eight by eight matrix featuring Sixty-Four Hexagrams. Each of the hexagrams had a commentary written by Wen Wang and the Duke of Zhou in about 1200 B.C., and this became the core of the text of the *I Ching* [Yi Jing] or *Book of Changes*.[4]

Underlying the hexagrams in the *Yi Jing* was the belief that, though the world was constantly changing, there was a supporting structure governing this process. The basic essence of this structure, according to Laozi, was the "Great Dao" which was intangible and indiscernible to normal people. Dao was

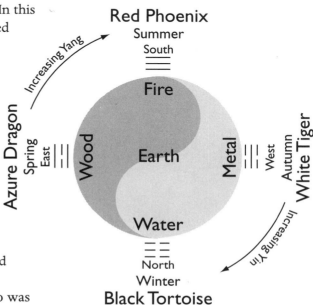

Earth-centered Trigram with its associations.

characterized by "Wu," or "Non-beingness," in a variety of ways. It was not only emptiness (Wu) but also nameless (Wuming), without desire (Wuyü), without action (Wu wei), without partiality (Wuxi), without limit (Wuji). The Dao did, however, have great power. If it was transformed into energy, for example, it became Qi. "Qi" literally meant the "air" or the "breath." As it was associated with intangible non-being, it was referred to as the "Cosmic Spirit."[5]

According to Daoist thought, this cosmic Qi that existed in the natural world also presented itself in the world of human beings. Human Qi, a form of life breath flowing through the acupuncture meridians of the body, was consistent with the Qi of the nature. The Chinese, Frena Bloomfield noted, "look upon nature not as a dead inanimate fabric, but as a living breathing organism. They see a golden chain of spiritual life running through every form of existence and binding together, as in one living body, everything that subsists on heaven above or on earth below."[6]

This view of a spiritual connection between the cosmos, the earth, and people that characterizes Chinese thought is particularly enlivening in view of the still-borne nature of much recent designing in the West. The specific nature of Daoist concepts such as Qi and Li, with their focus on the channeling of energy; Yin and Yang, or complementarity; and the implications of the ambiguous but central concept of "Non-being" will be explored in the context of the built environment in the sections that follow.

Qi and Li

Little, if any, explicit attention is paid in the West to the quality of the psychic energy in built environments. Some, like Le Corbusier, have made claims for the effect of a building's aesthetics on those who inhabit it.[7] Others, like Mies van der Rohe, with his reliance on Platonic geometry, have sought to create forms that "connect" to the cosmos through their geometric proportions.[8] But neither these, nor any other major approaches in Western design, have postulated the existence of an energy that flows through the natural environment and that must be harnessed in architecture if it is to be successful. The

Chinese concept of Qi is just such a force. Many definitions of Qi exist, but perhaps the most comprehensive is the following:

> Air, vapor, breath, ether, energy; also "temperament, strength, atmosphere"; central concept in Taoism [Daoism] and Chinese medicine. In the Taoist [Daoist] view ch'i [Qi] is the vital energy, the life force, the cosmic spirit that pervades and enlivens all things and is therefore synonymous with primordial energy.[9]

Qi represents energy, and, in the Chinese view, the dispersion of this energy was governed by fixed rules or laws of nature. These rules, which were called "Li," already existed prior to the first breath Qi. They included the principle of Yin and Yang, the cyclic movement of Five Elements and the Eight Trigrams, and the construction of Sixty-Four Hexagrams of the *Yi Jing*. The relationship of Qi to Li was clearly set out by Zhu Xi who noted:

> Throughout heaven and earth there is Li and there is Ch'i [Qi]. Li is the Tao [Dao] (organizing) all forms from above, and the root from which all things are produced. Ch'i [Qi] is the instrument (composing) all forms from below, and the tools and raw materials with which all things are made. Thus men and all other things must receive this Li at the moment of their coming into being, and thus get their specific nature; so also must they receive this Ch'i [Qi] and thus get their form.[10]

Qi, as expressed through the laws of Li, was the primary consideration in traditional Chinese architecture, and wind and water were the most important earthly forms carrying Qi. To describe this architecture as "vital" is not, then, just a metaphor. Rather, it is the very aim of all Chinese design to capture and channel the Qi which flows through the environment in a beneficial way. Qi rode the winds and dispersed, so that unprotected windy sites would lose any accumulated Qi. Still water, on the other hand, inhibited the flow of Qi, allowing it to become torpid or stagnant. To balance their effects, wind should be tamed to a gentle breeze to attract the circulating Qi, and flowing water should be curved and appropriately oriented to keep the Qi flowing, instead of allowing it to stagnate and become a malevolent force.[11]

The attempt to harness good Qi can clearly be seen in the Chinese landscape. The most favorable mountain landscape, for example, was generally believed to be the place where the two different types of Qi—one male (positive), the other one female (negative)—met and "copulated." The male Qi was present in the Azure Dragon mountain, which should be located to the east of a site. The female Qi was represented by the White Tiger mountain, which should be located to the west of the site. When two ridges of hills ran toward each other in a gentle curve and finally met each other at the northern portion of a site, the most favorable condition, true "Dragon Qi," would be generated. Taking another example, for positive flow of Qi on a site, water should flow slowly through sinuous and deep channels. Examples of these include "Immortal Palm" and "Palm Play Flute" water courses. Straight water courses in which water flows quickly conduct Qi away from the site rapidly and so are to be avoided. Overall, an ideal site was one protected from winds by a northern screen of hills or trees that was shaped in the form of an armchair. On this streams and rivers would meander slowly and, preferably, have a view to the south.

Consideration of the flow of Qi governed many formal aspects of Chinese architecture. For design at every scale—town planning, religious structures, houses, and gardens—sites were chosen and modified so that the effects of Dragon Qi could be enhanced and those of evil Qi could be diminished.

Immortal Palm and Palm Play water course.

Yin and Yang

Another principle that permeated Chinese thought and architecture was complementarity, represented by the relationship of Yin and Yang. This idea has been broached, wittingly and unwittingly, on occasion by architects in the West. The late formgiver Louis Kahn expressed it most clearly when discussing the design process for his Trenton Bath House. He noted:

> I discovered a very simple thing. I discovered that certain spaces are very unimportant and some spaces are the real raison d'etre for doing what you're doing. But the small

spaces were contributing to the strength of the larger
spaces. They were serving them.[12]

This is a key observation, often missed in the West where
we tend to think that every aspect of architecture should be a
grand gesture. Taking most cities and college campuses in the
United States as examples, what one tends to see is an abun-
dance of loud statements, with little dialogue to bring them
meaning or coherence. Instead, as Kahn realized, one must
conceive of a hierarchy of different types of space, each mutually supporting the other. This type of complementarity was
fundamental to the Chinese.

Traditionally in China different geometric forms were associated with the complementary forces of Yin and Yang. Heaven,
for example, was conceived of as a circle dominated by Yang
forces. The earth, in contrast, was square and was dominated
by Yin forces. Heaven, being Yang, symbolized vastness,
strength, power, motion, light, and solidity. The earth was associated with Yin whose attributes were meekness, weakness,
passivity, stillness, darkness, and voidness. The roundness of
heaven was diagrammatically represented above the earth by a
circle outside a square. So within the circle Yin and Yang forces
were not separated; they were more like the two opposite ends
of a pendulum swing—Yin forever gave way to Yang and Yang
to Yin in an eternal oscillation between the two poles.

In the Chinese architectural world buildings of all different
scales generally were constructed according to the rules of Li. It
is said that houses were built within the domain of the earth
and so were close to square in shape, while gardens were built
between the domains of heaven and earth. For capital cities,
imperial cities, and houses, for example, that geometry was
connected with the life of the earth. With imperial tombs and
gardens, however, in which the architecture was intended to
express human beings' relationship to heaven, a combination of
square and circular geometrical motifs were generally used.

Describing the presence of complementarity in Chinese
garden, Wing-Tsit Chan wrote:

> The Primeval Pair of the Yin and Yang, of the male and the
> female forces, the active and the passive principles, are faith-
> fully represented in hills and ponds, in stones and woods,
> and remind us of the harmony and order of the universe.
> The five elements of metal, wood, water, fire, and earth are

deeply religious to the Chinese because they unite all forms of existence into a network of correspondences so that thunder, wind, rain, air, and cloud have direct correspondence with the five directions which in turn act on the five metals, the five colors, the five organs of the human body and all other mentionable phenomena. . . . The Infinite and the finite are at every instance correlated. It is in this most fundamental sense that in the Chinese garden man and nature become one.[13]

The garden presents perhaps the clearest example of the oscillation between the Yin and Yang in the built environment. There one could sit all day contemplating metaphysical movements: some slow, some fast; some obvious, some obscure; some natural, some artificial. All of the patterns worked together to make manifest the fundamental principle of complementarity in the universe.

Non-being

The concepts of Qi and Li, energy and the laws by which it manifests itself, along with the principle of complementarity, as expressed through the opposition of Yin and Yang, illuminate ways of viewing the environment, and our interaction with it, that are almost wholly absent from Western design thinking. Though these concepts can be adapted for use by Western designers, perhaps the single most important idea in Chinese thought to consider as we seek to make design more responsive to nature, culture, and people is the very ambiguous notion of "Non-being," which is so central to Daoism.

Though it is difficult, if not impossible, to describe the essence of Non-being, John Chris Jones managed to capture its importance in the context of architecture. He wrote:

What can we learn from architecture? The old architecture. Buildings, places . . . places to be. As described by P'ei Ti [Pei Di], writing a thousand years ago, in China:

"In front of the balcony,
    as the expanse of water
    fills with ripples,
The solitary moon
    goes wandering without pause.
From the depth of the valley
    the cries of monkeys rise;
Borne by the wind
    they reach me in my room."

The building itself is barely mentioned. Yet its presence is felt. What is described, re-created, is the experience. Of being there, and of what else is there. The state of mind. Consisting of all these things. This, this so delicate awareness, is closer, I suppose, to "life," to what I'm now calling the new architecture, the architecture of being, of being here, of making the connections, for oneself.[14]

This sense of presence—of truly experiencing architecture, and not just architectural form—is what is so central in traditional Chinese architecture. The importance of this intangible quality of Non-being, or "the space in between," was clearly set out by Laozi in the fifth century B.C. He wrote:

Thirty spokes converge upon a single hub;
It is on the hole in the center that the use of the cart hinges.

We make a vessel from a lump of clay;
It is the empty space within the vessel that makes it useful.

We make doors and windows for a room;
But it is these empty spaces that make the room livable.

Thus, while the tangible has advantages,
It is the intangible that makes it useful.[15]

In the West we tend to focus, depending on our design disciplines, on the spokes and hubs, the lumps of clay, or the doors and windows. These are necessary elements, certainly, but we tend to limit ourselves to a consideration of the tangible in design to the near exclusion of the intangible. But, as Laozi's poem makes clear, usefulness is defined not by the tangible but by the intangible. The mismatches between designers' work and the contexts in which it is placed, which manifest themselves in every design discipline, can be traced to this fundamental misconception or, more accurately, misplacement of attention on the part of designers. Our true concern should be with the use of the cart, which is dependent on the hole in the hub; the vessel whose very nature is voidness; or the empty space defined by architectural elements, such as doors and windows—all examples of Daoist Non-being.

Through their focus on the tangible, designers effectively ignore the intangible qualities that actually make their work useful. This is certainly true in the traditional "object-oriented" design professions—urban planning, architecture, interior design, and product design—in which the overriding focus is on the arrangement of geometry. This emphasis on the tangible is less present in emerging areas, such as the design of computer operating systems and other software. In these cases the prime focus of design is not on physical artifacts, such as disks or manuals, but on the intangible processes by which the software will be used. The essence of high-technology design, in fact, is the experience that people have when "interfacing" with products. This is an area to which Eastern thought is particularly applicable.

Though it is rare for Non-being to be considered in application to more tangibly oriented design tasks, John Chris Jones did find the experience of design to be central to the work of Italian architect Sergio Los. Jones noted that Los spoke in a lecture of the:

> using and inhabiting of a building as a process, a physical process, differing only in scale from the physical process of constructing the building. In both processes materials and people move about over the site changing the positions and the forms of what is there. So, in this view, building is a form of living and living is a form of building. That's one way of realizing that there are no products, no fixities, only continuous flux. And that designing, making, and using are all processes that are added to, and interact with, the natural processes of the places where these activities occur.[16]

This quality of Los's work which Jones describes, that focuses on the use of space over time; on cyclical change; and on the importance of "the space in between," echoes the key features of Eastern thought. The significance of Eastern concepts such as Qi and Li, Yin and Yang, and Non-being to those of us in the West is that they provide us with cognitive tools through which to better understand the living quality of the world around us and, in turn, to better integrate ourselves with the patterns of activity and the forces that surround us.

3

Feng Shui

In recent years an increasing number of laypeople have taken an interest in the effect which the built environment has on them. The concerns that people have include the pragmatic, such as lack of comfort or proper accommodation of their activities; the visual, especially dissatisfaction with sterile and unappealing surroundings; health issues, including sick building syndrome and carpal tunnel syndrome; and the more far-fetched such as fear of malevolent spirits that endanger physical and mental health.

A single subject—Feng Shui (pronounced "fung shway")—seems to encompass all of these concerns, and in recent years there has been an enormous number of books published on this topic.[1] The books themselves range from the authoritative to the highly speculative, the latter perhaps justifying their placement on the library shelf between those on Tarot reading and numerology. Whatever the limitations of the present Feng Shui fad in the West, the subject must be examined seriously because it provides the longest-standing framework through which Eastern philosophical ideas are incorporated into design. Feng Shui principles affect everything from the siting of buildings and the structural systems used in architecture, to the placement of furniture and the choice of interior colors. In this chapter, definitions of Feng Shui will be reviewed, and examples of its application will be cited. The current practice of Feng Shui will be briefly surveyed, and the applicability of this approach to Western design will be assessed.

Defining Feng Shui

Feng Shui had been practiced in China since ancient times. Government buildings, palaces, and temples have been constructed in accordance with the principles of Feng Shui for over 3,000 years. In addition to this type of official work, Feng Shui practitioners were also called upon by the Chinese before they started construction of new houses or chose burial sites for the dead. As a result, Feng Shui has underpinned the pattern of development of the entire Chinese landscape.

As noted in the previous chapter, traditionally the Chinese consider Qi to be a living form of energy animating everything in the universe. The ancient Chinese developed different techniques to manipulate the flow of Qi for the benefit of human beings. Perhaps the best known of these methods to Westerners is the practice of acupuncture, in which the flow of Qi is modified by locating and stimulating the acupuncture meridian points. Feng Shui is similar to acupuncture but manifests itself at the scale of the environment. In this case the flow of Qi is manipulated by making changes to the surface of the earth, and to structures located on it. Feng Shui literally means "wind and water." It is so named after the two most important sources of flowing Qi on the earth.

With a topic as broad and ambiguous as Feng Shui, perhaps the best way to develop an understanding of it is to present a range of views of the subject. One of the earliest Westerners to write about Feng Shui was Christian missionary Ernest J. Eitel in 1873. In explaining the belief system that Feng Shui was based on, he noted of the Chinese that "they see a golden chain of spiritual life running through every form of existence and binding together, as in one living body, everything that subsists in heaven above or on earth below."[2] John Michell, in introducing a contemporary edition of Eitel's *Feng Shui*, develops this notion further:

> All who have written about it agree that feng-shui recognizes, besides the palpable elements such as wind and water, certain types of energy which permeate the earth and atmosphere and animate the forms of nature; but further understanding has been blocked by the impossibility of equating these energies with phenomena recognized by modern physics. . . . Whereas the modern tendency is to

separate these energies and concepts into different categories, the Chinese regarded the invisible side of nature as a
whole, and formulated in feng-shui a code of practice to
govern their relations to it. The geological, atmospheric and
psychic qualities of every potential building site were
assessed together by one science, which determined the
position and planning of all houses and types of construction
throughout China.[3]

The origin of Feng Shui was addressed by Sarah Rossbach in
her book *Feng Shui: The Chinese art of placement*. She explained:

> For all the mystery that surrounds it, feng shui evolved from
> the simple observation that people are affected, for good
> and ill, by surroundings: the layout and orientation of work-
> places and homes. In addition, the Chinese have long
> observed that some surroundings are better, luckier, or
> more blessed than others. Every hill, building, wall, window,
> and corner and the ways in which they face wind and water
> have an effect. They concluded that if you change surround-
> ings, you can change your life. The aim of feng shui, then, is
> to change and harmonize the environment—cosmic cur-
> rents known as *ch'i* [Qi]—to improve fortunes.[4]

With a subject as ancient as Feng Shui, and one that was
handed down orally for centuries before being systematized,
there will inevitably be ambiguities and inconsistencies between
accounts. Whatever the differences, however, and no matter
how far-fetched some of the contemporary writing on the subject is, the purpose of Feng Shui is to enable people to live in
better harmony with the natural environment and the cosmos
—a worthwhile goal, if nothing else.

Feng Shui practice

Traditionally the practice of Feng Shui can be divided into two
principal categories: the Form School and the Compass School.
The Form School is based largely on a consideration of land
forms and terrain, in particular mountains and water courses.

Practitioners of the Compass School, not surprisingly perhaps, use a compass, called a "lopan," to help decide upon sites and orientations for buildings. Though the theory on which use of the lopan is based is very arcane, involving a complex mathematical system, its application is actually more mechanical and straightforward than the practices of the Form School. Despite their differences, both the Form School and the Compass School have the same intention—to "tap into" the same Li principles, the central notion of which is that the universe possesses wholeness.[5]

Though both the Form and Compass schools of Feng Shui address the siting and forms of the built environment and their relationship to traditional Chinese philosophies and belief systems, current Feng Shui practice in the West tends to have a more limited focus. There is great popular interest in Feng Shui at the moment; however, the majority of applications in the West involve small-scale interventions in the environment that are intended simply to redirect the flow of Qi within an existing space. The limitations of much of what is written on Feng Shui in the West is reflected by the following passage from one of the better-known writers on the subject, Evelyn Lip. In her book *Feng Shui for business*, she gives designers the following advice:

> The commercial building must appeal to the visitor's emotional reactions. The customer must feel comfortable and relaxed. For example, a restaurant should have conducive lighting with absolutely no glare, soothing colour scheme and a temperature level which is not too hot or too cold.[6]

Though it is hard to disagree with her suggestions, they are not particularly profound, nor do they reflect the quality of the Chinese philosophies that underpin Feng Shui. Unfortunately, however, this level of generality is typical of much of the popular writing on the subject.

Norman Foster and Associates. The Headquarters of the Hongkong and Shanghai Banking Corporation Limited, 1985. Exterior view from Statue Square. *(Photo courtesy of the Hongkong and Shanghai Banking Corporation Limited)*

Applications of Feng Shui

Contemporary Feng Shui practice in the Far East encompasses a much greater scope than its Western counterpart. Feng Shui has been used to guide the design and construction of buildings throughout Asia. Even today in Taiwan, Hong Kong, and Singapore, most modern developments have Feng Shui aspects. In Singapore, for example, a block of public housing flats had to be structurally changed because their front doors faced each other—a bad omen in terms of Feng Shui. People refused to move into the building until the door position was changed. In Hong Kong, the new Regent Hotel was designed with a large glass atrium through which the entire harbor could be seen. This was done so that the wide sweep of the harbor was not obstructed, in accordance with the requirements of good Feng Shui practice.[7]

One of the most publicized Feng Shui applications in Asia was to the massive new building for the Hongkong and Shanghai Banking Corporation, designed by Britain's Sir Norman Foster in the high-tech style and reputed to be the world's most expensive building.[8] One of the building's notable features is that the entire skyscraper is lifted off the ground so that people can walk under it (this is intended as a bit of "muscle flexing" to highlight the strength of the building's exposed structure). It is ironic, then, that part of the design for this demonstration piece of Western, rationalist design was influenced, at the client's insistence, by a Feng Shui practitioner. Lung King Chuen, a geomancer, was chosen to advise the bank on the project. The late British essayist Bruce Chatwin addressed the importance of Feng Shui practitioners such as Chuen in his essay "The Chinese Geomancer." He wrote:

> The business of the geomancer is to make certain, with the help of a magnetic compass, that a building, a room, a grave or a marriage-bed is aligned to one or other of the "dragon-lines" and shielded from dangerous cross-currents. Without clearance from a *feng-shui* expert, even the most "westernised" Chinese businessman is apt to get the jitters, to say nothing of his junior staff.[9]

Chatwin set out Lung King Chuen's specific role in the design of the new Hongkong and Shanghai Bank building as follows:

> At the start of the project, the Bank called him in to survey the site for malign or demonic presences, and to ensure that the design itself was propitious. Whichever architect was

Norman Foster and Associates. The Headquarters of the Hongkong and Shanghai Banking Corporation Limited, **1985.** View of plaza. *(Photo courtesy of the Hongkong and Shanghai Banking Corporation Limited)*

Norman Foster and Associates. The Headquarters of the Hongkong and Shanghai Banking Corporation Limited, **1985.** View of atrium. *(Photo courtesy of the Hongkong and Shanghai Banking Corporation Limited)*

chosen, there was bound to be some anxiety; for the Hongkong and Shanghai Bank is the pivot on which Hong Kong itself stands or falls.[10]

Chatwin was then guided on a tour of the completed building by Chuen, who pointed out one of the changes he had suggested in order to bring the design into conformance with good Feng Shui practice. The Feng Shui man had "recommended that the escalator to the first floor—which was, after all, the main public entrance—should be so angled, obliquely, that it ran along a 'dragon-line.'"[11] This was significant because, as Chatwin explained:

> From the most ancient times the Chinese have believed that the Earth is a mirror of the Heavens, and that both are living sentient beings shot through and through with currents of energy—some positive, some negative—like the messages that course through our own central nervous systems.
> These positive currents—those carrying good "chih" [zhi], or "life force"—are known as "dragon-lines". They are thought to follow the flow of underground water, and the direction of magnetic fields beneath the Earth's surface.[12]

Though Chuen was somewhat reticent to talk about it, there were aspects in the final design that were not in conformance with good Feng Shui practice. As Chatwin relates:

> Finally, Mr. Lung said, he had to admit there were a number of danger zones in the structure—"killing-points" is what he called them—where, in order to counteract negative chih [zhi], it had been necessary to station living plants: a potted palm at the head of the escalator "in case of a fall"; more potted palms by the lift-shafts; yet more palms close to the pylons to nullify the colossal downward thrust of the building.[13]

The practice of Feng Shui is based on the notion that masters of the subject are more intuitively "tuned into" the psychic energy of an environment than are laypeople. Whatever its strengths or weaknesses, and however true or false the principles it is based on, Feng Shui does in fact govern the design of many buildings in Asia, as Western architects soon find out when working there. In an article in *Progressive Architecture*, Philip Langdon addressed this situation. He noted:

Many designers in Asia have responded to the local culture by applying feng shui, the Chinese art of placement, to the design and siting of buildings. Feng shui holds that some locations and shapes are auspicious while others are likely to bring misfortune. Buildings influenced by feng shui are usually laid out with their most important spaces facing south. Symmetry is considered desirable. Often buildings are constructed in pairs—not slipping past each other, like New York's World Trade center towers, but closely aligned. Certain shapes, such as a fish profile, appear frequently. The five-story atrium of Kohn Pedersen Fox's big Nanjing Xi Lu mixed-use project on the main commercial street in Shanghai has a fish-shaped plan. Certain numbers, such as eight, are considered lucky; many Chinese highrises are articulated in eight story increments.

Symbolism [also] plays an important role. For instance, the Shekou Harbor Building near Shenzhen, designed by Chicago's Loebl Schlossman and Hackl, will display a sail-like shape across much of its 40-story curtain wall and will have a plan like that of a ship, to recall the countless junks that have sailed past its site in the Pearl River basin.[14]

When designing for Asian clients in the United States, architects must also be sensitive to Feng Shui principles, as Paul Glanzrock noted of the design of China Trust bank's New York offices:

Unlike American banks, China Trust's clientele share a distinctly unified cultural heritage—honoring such heritage has been a primary concern. "In Taiwan and China, generally, people do their business where they feel comfortable," says [client representative Fu S.] Mei. "We wanted to emphasize that not only could we provide the expertise of a full-service, modern bank, but that we were also part of the community, and would go out of our way to satisfy our customers' personal needs," Mei says.

In keeping with this approach, the bank is a synthesis of new and old. An exterior of white metal, glass, and chrome houses an interior influenced by a 3,000-year old Chinese design tradition called Feng Shui. . . . Somewhere between numerology and interior design by Western standards, Feng Shui is a complex system that divines how the shape and attributes of any building (no matter how elaborate or simple) will affect the fortunes of its inhabitants (residential or business). "In China, Feng Shui is as basic as architecture itself," says Mei. "Management made it clear they wanted the tradition upheld in New York." The water fountain in the atrium, for example, has flowing water (traditionally associated with good business in China) to offset the inauspicious corner entrance way, which mimics the end of an arrow or sharp point.

Feng Shui has been adapted by many Asian businesses, particularly restaurants. Sometimes, a Feng Shui expert will prescribe radical structural changes, such as the moving of an entranceway around a corner, or the installation of a double door—incurring hefty expenses. By conducting the assessment early in the design phase, China Trust incurred no such "adjustments" (excepting the fountain, which cost about $50,000). "Luckily, the Feng Shui expert prescribed a fountain only six inches deep," says [architect Joseph] Tarella, "or else the city would have considered it a swimming pool."[15]

Though Feng Shui is a major force in Asia, and with Asian clients, its use in the United States by Westerners tends to be restricted in scale and scope to "the art of placement." Most applications simply involve the placement of crystals and mirrors that are intended to direct Qi within an interior space, rather than having it govern the siting and design of buildings themselves.

An assessment of Feng Shui

Although Feng Shui is widely accepted to have validity in Asia, few, if any, of the claims made for its efficacy could ever be proven scientifically. But, for us, this isn't the key question. Instead, we are interested in determining if Feng Shui principles are useful for designers who want to create a more humane, wholistic environment. We are also curious about what has led to the delirious praise and attention that this approach has received in recent years. It is, of course, impossible to be definitive but, having studied and worked with this approach closely, we will present our critical assessment of present-day Feng Shui practice, especially in terms of its relevance for the West.

Is there a latent energy in the natural and built environment? Certainly. Do Western designers fail to account for this in their work? Without a doubt. *But,* this does not mean that all of the anecdotal evidence of Feng Shui "success" reported in popular books on the subject is to believed. The attraction of most Feng Shui books, as our colleague and friend Ron Mowat says, is that they provide *an* answer and, in a world full of ambiguity, this can be very attractive to people. One of the most difficult points to get across to introductory students is that while, in a complex subject such as design, there is no one right answer, there are many wrong ones—anything that purports to be the answer in any design field is bound to be wrong, or at least incomplete. The same is true of Feng Shui.

What certainly seems wrong is the idea that Westerners who import the forms and artifacts of another culture, without adopting its belief and value system, will experience the same results that are found in its original context. The "magical" results of Feng Shui application probably have less to do with design per se than with faith in what the design represents. This point can, perhaps, be best understood through the following traditional Buddhist parable: Three sets of beings approach a stream. The first group is from the god realm. They stop and assess the contents of the stream and conclude that it is filled with pure nectar. The second group consists of people from the human realm. Their assessment? Pure water. The third group are hungry ghosts, lower-realm beings who search for years, without success, to find water and food. Their view of the stream contents? Puss and blood, which is all they are ever destined to find in their journeys.[16] The point of this story in the context of Feng Shui is simple—if people have an understanding of and belief in the principles of Feng Shui, and the philosophies that underpin it, as many contemporary Asians do, then it is real to them. If, on the other hand, those same forms are used in a setting where the people do not share that belief system, then they have no power—they do not experience the same results, even in an ostensibly similar situation. In other words, what you see when observing a situation depends upon what your beliefs are before you look at it.

Another explanation for the reports of Feng Shui positively affecting the lives of those who have employed it might be the so called "Hawthorne Effect." In 1924 the managers of the

Western Electric Company, whose workers assembled telephone equipment, wanted to increase morale and productivity at their plant in Chicago. The management decided to alter the quality and quantity of the lighting in the factory to see if that helped—they were looking for *the* level of illumination that would make their workers most productive. The studies themselves were quite involved, but in summary form what happened was that management increased the lighting levels and, as a result, productivity went up. Just to confirm their result they reduced lighting levels to their original level and, surprisingly enough, productivity levels did not decrease.[17] The management, after further studies, realized that it was not the lighting levels themselves that were affecting productivity but the perception on the part of the workers that management, by experimenting with the lighting, was doing something *for them*. Most Feng Shui "successes" reported in the West, it seems clear, are Hawthorne effects—people are responding to the fact that they themselves, or someone acting on their behalf, has taken a direct interest in, and exerted control over, their immediate environment.

Another contributing factor to reports of its success could be the fact that Feng Shui addresses a scale of design—an immediacy—that the design professions, even interior design, tend to overlook. Also of significance is that Feng Shui design decisions are governed by human interest, not aesthetic theory, and so the results tend to be perceived by people as being more comfortable than those provided by professional designers. There are, in short, many reasons why people would respond favorably to Feng Shui interventions that do not rely on the "magical" explanations resorted to in some of the popular writing on the subject.

But what of the "magical" explanations? Where do they come from? Another friend, British design historian Andrew King, addressed this in terms of Qi, the principle underlying all Feng Shui work. He noted:

> The Chinese belief in Qi seems to be very real, but to what extent the concept is a metaphor, and to what extent it is an explanatory mechanism for phenomena, similar, for example, to the concept of electricity, is interesting. Qi is evidently a useful concept or "thinking tool" to manipulate understanding of certain kinds of mental/physical practices and phenomena. But its relation to experience *may* be that

of a "magical" rather than a "rational" cognitive model, by which I mean that many evidently bizarre cognitive models recounted by practitioners of religion or magic often apparently lead to highly efficacious behaviour in the real world, not because they explain the real world accurately in the "scientific" sense, or because they model reality sufficiently well to ensure efficacious behaviour. The point is that in most cases, and often in science itself, behaviour is evolved first and explanations are developed afterwards.[18]

King's assessment is probably as close as one can come to "explaining" Feng Shui. It is not, as some of the advocates for it claim, a comprehensive theory of interaction with the world. Rather, it is a belief system that has evolved over the centuries and which contains a lot of useful folk knowledge about how to make environments work for people. In other words, there are a lot of very useful pieces of the system, though the system itself as a whole probably is not "valid" in Western terms. Though there are many reasons to doubt the claims often made for Feng Shui, experience shows that it *can*, in fact, be useful. We reserve the last words in this critical survey for Bruce Chatwin who acknowledges that:

> we all feel that some houses are "happy" and others have a "nasty atmosphere." Only the Chinese have come up with cogent reasons why this should be so. Whoever presumes to mock *feng-shui* as a superstitious anachronism should recall its vital contribution to the making of the Chinese landscape, in which houses, temples and cities were always sited in harmony with trees and hills and water.
>
> Perhaps one can go a step further? Perhaps the *rootedness* of Chinese civilisation; the Chinese sense of belonging to the Earth; their capacity to live without friction in colossal numbers—have all, in the long run, resulted from their adherence to the principles of *feng-shui*?[19]

4

Dao in Design

An examination of Daoist principles in design is useful for Western designers, not so much to learn about the actual forms of the Chinese landscape, architecture, and design but in order to become familiar with the ideas that have stimulated their development. Through study of the overriding concepts that animate this living tradition, we in the West can learn how to infuse our own designs with a more humane quality. The aspects of traditional Chinese architecture that could prove to be of particular importance to Westerners include the following:

1. Developing an awareness of the flow of psychic energy, the experiential quality, or, to put it in the vernacular, the "vibe" of spaces
2. Gaining an understanding of the presence of symbolism and of forms whose meanings are shared across a culture
3. Addressing the spiritual, as well the pragmatic, aspects of space
4. Considering the harmony of buildings, landscape, and nature
5. Learning about the integration of designing with the patterns of everyday life
6. Adopting a concern with the impact of design on ecological systems of all types

The design context that perhaps most clearly illustrates these principles, and the way in which they work together, is

The Pavilion in the Nanjing Friendship Garden at the Missouri Botanical Gardens, St. Louis. *(Courtesy of the Missouri Botanical Gardens)*

Handcarved white marble bridge in the Nanjing Friendship Garden at the Missouri Botanical Gardens, St. Louis. *(Photo: Peggy Kelly, courtesy of the Missouri Botanical Gardens)*

the garden. The relationship of people to the results of design activity was beautifully expressed by Wing-Tsit Chan in his essay "Man and Nature in the Chinese Garden." He wrote:

> How is fellowship of man and nature possible in the garden? The answer lies in the fact that the garden is a harmonious display of the very vitality of both man and nature. This is rhythm, which, to the Chinese, is the highest of all conceivable values, the quintessence of truth, beauty, and goodness of the highest levels of existence. In the realm of philosophy, it is Tao [Dao] or the Way. In the realm of religion it is the Cosmic Soul. In the realm of art it is Universal Breath. Chinese religion and philosophy become unintelligible as soon as the element of rhythm is removed, for whether spoken of as the Way or Tao [Dao], it is at bottom the universal principle of the harmony of the Yin (the female) and the Yang (the male) principles, or the negative and the positive forces of the universe.[1]

Addressing the visual quality of the garden, Chan explains:

> Formalism and regularity . . . entirely disappear from the garden. The keynote of arrangements, whether of rockeries, gates, paths, or flower beds, is irregularity. Formality is sacrificed

in favor of informality. Both the straight line and the sharp corner are dispensed with, to such a degree that the entire garden becomes a diffusion of curves. . . . Geometric arrangements are abhorred because both the geometric pattern of thought and the geometric pattern of life limit the freedom of the spirit.

This freedom is not to be conceived as careless, orderless, irresponsible activity. It is freedom within a prescribed order. Nature is never looked upon by the Chinese as chaotic or disorganized. Heaven and earth co-exist in harmony, and the four seasons run their course regularly. Thus the Confucians and the Taoists [Daoists] unite in reminding the Chinese that there is a universal principle pervading all things, whether in the realm of physical nature or in the sphere of human life. . . . In casting away regularity in favor of irregularity for his garden, the Chinese never violates the regularity of nature. . . . Over and above irregularity and informality, there reigns a higher order, the order of nature.[2]

The solution to our present dilemma of poor-quality design in the West is not simply to build Chinese gardens ourselves, however. Rather, we need to adopt the qualities that Chan so eloquently describes—the sense that we are not just designing for ourselves but instead are relating our work to the patterns of the cosmos. The formalism and regularity that are the hallmarks of Western design theories give way, in the Chinese garden, to a focus on integration with, and honoring of, nature. Whereas Western design (and thought in general) has consisted of a brave resistance, but ultimate capitulation, to the fundamental forces at play in the universe, Chinese design has not been so arrogant. There is no attempt to do the impossible—to "subdue" nature, as in the "heroic" West. Rather, they have sought to integrate themselves, as thoroughly and as best they could, into the patterns by which the universe operates. They are not merely "symbolizing" nature, or using it as "thematic material," as some style trends in the West have done. The ancient Chinese were, through their design interventions, literally trying to take their place in nature.

In order to demonstrate this highly complex interweaving of philosophical belief and built form, a visual survey will be presented featuring four different scales of designing: town planning, religious structures, houses, and gardens. At each scale different design tasks will be reviewed in order to demonstrate the formal

Tai Hu stones and stream in the Nanjing Friendship Garden at the Missouri Botanical Gardens, St. Louis. (Photo: Jack Jennings, courtesy of the Missouri Botanical Gardens)

ideas being employed and the ideas that underpin them. To illustrate these points, reference will be made not only to examples from Chinese architectural history but also to the design of an unbuilt prototype, the Village of Long Happiness. This design, by Jiangmei Wu, is based on traditional principles and the vernacular forms of the Fujian province of southern China. It was created in order to make the interrelationships between form and philosophy as clear as possible to the reader.

As noted earlier, it is not the intention of this book to serve as a how-to guide to Daoist design, nor is it a history of Chinese architecture, per se. Moreover, there has been no attempt made to address specific functional issues that would have to be accounted for in a working design in the visual survey. Instead, the aim is to show how, in traditional Chinese designing at all scales, form and cultural meaning are inextricably linked. We hope that through this presentation the reader can develop an intuitive "feel" for how Western design might be rethought in order to give it the living, responsive quality that characterizes design based on Daoist thought.

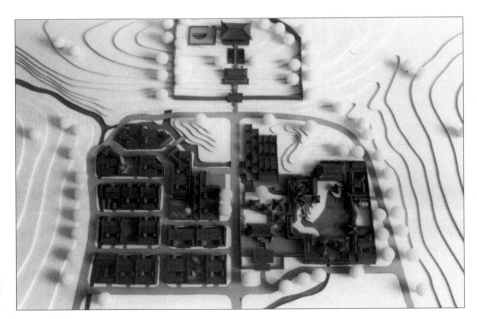

Aerial view of the
Village of Long Happiness
(model).

Town planning

We will begin our presentation of the ideas that underpin traditional Chinese architecture and design by looking at the largest scale—town planning—in terms of the design decisions made in the planning of the Village of Long Happiness. At this scale the main concerns were choosing a site; locating the neighborhoods and the individual houses within them; and the arrangement of a comprehensive community center including gardens, a commercial area, a school, and an ancestral temple. The presentation of the village's design will follow a linear sequence, setting out the nature of each of the individual patterns that were used to guide the design process.

SITE SELECTION

The first consideration was the choice of site. According to Feng Shui principles, a site surrounded by mountains in a horseshoe shape is best. The mountain to the north should be the highest one in the area, and the slope to the south should be very gentle. The mountain to the east is called the Dragon Mountain, and the one to the west the Tiger Mountain. According to Chinese beliefs, the Dragon Mountain is dominated by the Yang force, and in the Tiger Mountain the Yin force is predominant. When the Yin and the Yang forces meet, they produce an incredible energy that is thought to be of benefit to the site, and to its inhabitants.

Mountains and water always co-exist. Running water is considered a Yang force, and serene mountains have a Yin association. The best water courses carry Dragon Qi and are called, not surprisingly, Dragon water courses. These should meander through the landscape, and the rate of flow of the water in the river should be very slow. Running water is said to touch the river bank just like a hand playing a flute; in the middle of the palm of this imaginary hand Dragon Qi is thought to gather. This was chosen as the cardinal point of the site.

Historically, these same issues were considered when choosing a site. An example of consideration of Qi in choosing the site for a capital city is found in Jiankang. The city was surrounded by mountains and hills on three sides, with the northern, western, and eastern mountains joining together to

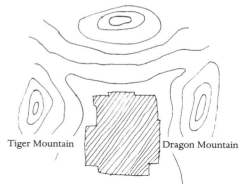

Site diagram of the Village of Long Happiness showing the relationship of the armchair-shaped mountain ranges to the living space.

Tiger Mountain   Dragon Mountain

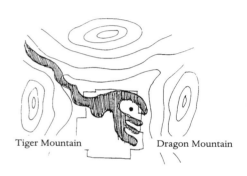

Tiger Mountain   Dragon Mountain

Site diagram of the Village of Long Happiness showing the Dragon Water course and the cardinal point where Qi gathers.

Site plan of Jiankang, showing the northern lake from which water flowed through the site.

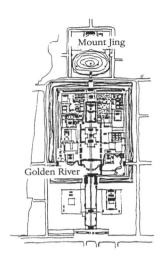

Site plan of Beijing's Forbidden City, showing the artificial mountain constructed to the north of the site.

form the auspicious shape of an armchair. It was believed that armchair-shaped mountain ranges could protect the city by preventing the dispersal of beneficial Qi. At Jiankang, in addition, water courses flowed from the northern lake and meandered to the south of the city, allowing Qi to accumulate without becoming stagnant.

The siting of buildings of imperial cities and palaces was also given great attention. Imperial cities were usually located within the inner layers of city walls. While the city itself might not possess many different natural features, an artificial landscape could be created to give rise to beneficial Qi. The imperial city of Beijing, known as the "Forbidden City," demonstrates this practice. At the northern end of the axis, where the most important buildings are located, an artificial mountain called "Mount Jing" was built to provide protection to the north of the imperial palace. To the south of the city an artificial water course, called "the Golden River," meandered in the front of the palace. The Golden River was built to simulate the qualities of ideal natural water courses.

View of the Golden River in Beijing's Forbidden City, an artificial water course built to simulate the quality of a slowly flowing natural river.

STREET LAYOUT

The layout of Chinese streets is usually symmetrical. The main street of the Village of Long Happiness was located on the central north-south axis of the site. When the main street leads to an important building, such as an ancestral temple, it can, as in this case, be called "the Spirit Road." The overall layout of the streets in the village followed a grid-like arrangement. This

View of housing clusters in the Village of Long Happiness (model).

grid was chosen to be consistent with the square wall surrounding the village and to symbolize the square earth. The grid was, however, altered in order to adapt to the topography of the site and to its special landscape features.

The central consideration of Feng Shui—the flow of Qi—was also reflected in the layout of every aspect of cities historically, especially in the design of the streets and residual spaces. The streets of the city are thought to be analogous to the acupuncture meridians of the human body—the intersection of streets being similar to acupuncture points and therefore requiring special attention. For example, no building should be built at the end of a long running street to guard against injuries from malevolent Qi (it was believed that evil Qi ran in straight lines). Instead, special monumental structures, such as a drum tower or a bell tower, were built at the end of the main streets that ran from south to north, or at the intersections of main streets, in order to modify the speed of Qi. In Beijing, for example, at the intersection of the main axial street and the main street running from east to west, a drum tower and a bell tower were built. The same pattern could be found in the plan of the city of Xi'an; at the intersection of the two main streets of the city a drum tower was built, with a bell tower close to it. These examples are not exceptional. Almost every Chinese city traditionally had a drum tower or a bell tower built at the crossing of the main streets. This even occurred in small towns, such as Tai Gu in Shanxi.

The classic text on the layout of Chinese cities was named *Kaogongji*,[3] and was, it is believed, written during the Warring States period (481 to 221 B.C.). Most "new" cities were developed according to the rules of city planning set out in the *Kaogongji*. This prescribed that Chinese capital cities could either be square or rectangular in shape, with the imperial city located to the north of the site. In certain cases it was more difficult to formally accommodate these beliefs. The secondary capital city Luoyang, for example, was built on a special landscape. The river Luo flowed through the middle part of the city, and, though the site had a complicated landscape, the city was still built on a square. The imperial city,

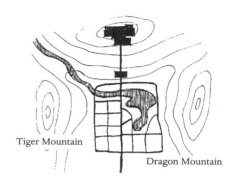

Diagram of the layout of the Village of Long Happiness's major streets.

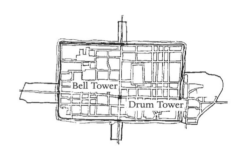

Street structure of Xi'an, showing drum and bell towers.

Perspective view of the Main Street and Drum Tower at Tai Gu in the Shanxi province.

Distant view of the Main Street and Drum Tower at Tai Gu in the Shanxi province.

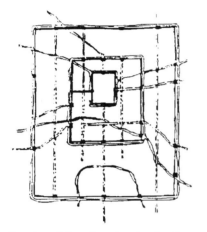

Site plan of Dongjing, showing the three sets of major enclosure walls.

which was also square in shape, was located to the northwest. The capital city Dongjing is another example of the square plan. The city itself had three separate sets of square-shaped enclosure walls, and the imperial city was also built toward the northern portion of the city and was located within the inner set of walls. The capital city Dadu was built on a plain. As is traditional, the city was square in shape with a very regular gridded street layout. In this case, however, the imperial city was located in the southern part of the city instead of to the north. One reason for this might be that the rulers of the Yuan dynasty were originally the nomadic people from the north who did not fully accept Chinese philosophical beliefs.

Some city development was deeply influenced by the forms already in place. Beijing provides an example of this. The new site for the city was adjacent to the site of the capital of the Yuan dynasty. This resulted in a plan of irregular shape, with the imperial city relocated to the northern part of the new city. This shift corrected the mistake found in the previous city near the site, Dadu. The new axis of Beijing ran from south to north with many monumental gates carefully placed along its length to define it. Beijing provides an archetypal example of how to locate an imperial city. Within the square walls of the city the imperial city is located to the north, in order to correspond to the location of the Pole Star—the cardinal point of the heavens —in the sky. It was thought that the imperial city should be located on the cardinal axis, the heavenly meridian, and that the emperor who, it was believed, was at the apex of the earthly hierarchy, should sit to the north and face south. Like the Pole Star, his enlightened spirit was to be shared by the four quarters of the earth. Outside of the square wall of the Forbidden City itself, four altars were located: the Altars of Heaven (south), Earth (north), Moon (west), and Sun (east).

The numbers nine and three are consistent themes in the book *Kaogongji,* especially in relationship to capital cities. The symbolic use of numbers was also found in the design and planning of imperial cities. The Forbidden City in Beijing provides a good example of this—the design strictly followed ancient rules. The city itself was close to square in shape with a gate in each of the four side walls. The four gates were associated with the four quarters of the earth. On each of the four corners of the walls a tower was built; these symbolic uses of the number four were thought to bring peacefulness. The city was symmetrically designed with a balance of Yin and Yang forces. On the central axis of the Forbidden City were three main palaces and five monumental gates; the numbers three and five were associated with imperial power.

These three main palaces were named "Taihedian" (the Palace of Supreme Harmony), "Zhonghedien" (the Palace of Central Harmony), and "Baohedian" (the Palace of Preserving Harmony). Each of these palaces was built on terraces at different levels and constructed of white granite. The greatest among the palaces is the Taihedian, where the most important ceremonies were held. The Taihedian featured a double-layered Wutien (curved) roof. These roofs are among the most hierarchically important elements in Chinese architecture. The palace itself had a symmetrical layout and, at the northern end of the axis, the throne of the emperor was located.

Site plan of Dadu, showing the imperial city to the south of the site.

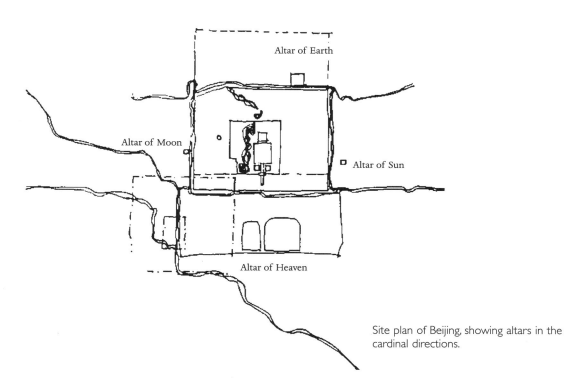

Site plan of Beijing, showing altars in the cardinal directions.

FUNCTIONAL ZONING

The four principal types of space within the Village of Long Happiness are the religious temple, the garden, houses, and the commercial area. Of these, the religious temple has the greatest significance. The temple was located on the top of the highest mountain of this district: The northern mountain. It overlooks

View of the Village of Long Happiness showing housing clusters (model).

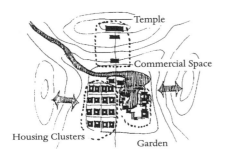

Diagram of functional zoning for the Village of Long Happiness.

Diagram of the flow of the seasons, as represented in the Village of Long Happiness's housing cluster gardens.

the entire village. The houses and the garden were to the west and east of the site according to their respective Yin and Yang qualities. It is generally believed that activities should be matched to the areas in the landscape that share their qualities. Living requires calmness and is associated with Yin; thus the dwellings were built near the Tiger Mountain to the west that is linked to that force. Gardening, on the other hand, is thought to be a Yang activity, so the garden was built near the Dragon Mountain to the east. The garden's location also incorporates a large body of water—one of the most important elements in any Chinese garden. The commercial area is located centrally, near the back of the dwellings. In some areas where the land is expensive, private commercial spaces are combined with dwellings.

There are four housing clusters within the living community. Each housing cluster consists of four to six houses and a small garden. The clusters are named after the gardens found within them. The gardens themselves are named after the four seasons in order to symbolize the flow of the four seasons into one another, and the flow of universal Qi. Each garden is located at the center of a housing cluster and was designed according to motifs related to the season it is associated with. The Garden of Spring, for example, has a rock in the shape of a bamboo shoot and live bamboo plants. Fresh bamboo shoots come out only during the spring, and so they are a symbol of that season. The Garden of Spring housing cluster is located to the east of the site as spring is symbolically associated with that direction. The Garden of Summer contains a water pond that is intended to reflect the blue sky characteristic of that season. The pool in the garden is also thought to give people a feeling of coolness. The Garden of Summer is located to the south of the site, in accordance with the season's symbolic association. The Garden of Autumn contains rocks of a golden brown color and is planted with Chinese maples, whose leaves turn a red-gold color during the fall. Golden colors are symbolically associated with autumn, as is the Western direction in which the housing cluster is located. Pine trees are planted in the Garden of Winter, and rocks with many cavities are placed in the garden. The cavities within the rocks allow the chilly winter wind to pass through. This is intended to enhance the feeling of the severity of the coldness of the weather. This cluster is located to the north of the site in keeping with Chinese symbolism for winter.

Religious structures

Having decided upon the overall layout of the Village of Long Happiness, attention was next turned to the single most important part of the village—the religious structures. The dominant feature of this complex is the Ancestral Temple which was located on the top of the hill to the north of the village. The temple serves to terminate the axis defined by the Spirit Road, an imaginary line that extends south to north through the center of town. The use of symbolism, though important in all traditional Chinese architecture, has particular significance in application to religious structures.

SPIRIT ROADS, TEMPLES, AND MONASTERIES

The design of the temple complex as a whole was oriented around the Spirit Road and includes the Heaven Gate, the Heaven Stairway, the Temple Buildings, and the Heaven Pond on the top of the hill. The layout of the temple is symmetrical, and all the important elements are located on an axis defined by the Spirit Road. The Spirit Road itself extends from the south of the village to the foot of the hill to the north on which the temple stands. The road serves to connect two worlds: the ordinary

View of the Village of Long Happiness's Spirit Road, leading up to the Ancestral Temple *(model)*.

View of the Village of Long Happiness's Ancestral Temple *(model)*.

physical world and the world as understood in Daoist religion. At the entrance to the Spirit Road a gate is located that consists of a pair of stone towers named "Que." These towers are built to symbolize the "pillar of heaven" and consist of tablet-like stone towers covered with eaves and ridges. This structure is supported by "Tou Kung," or Chinese brackets. In addition, pairs of stone animals stand on either side of the road; these are believed to be heavenly guards. The motifs chosen include lions, tigers, elephants, horses, and other animals.

At the first gate of the temple complex, the Spirit Road changes into a stairway, called the "Heaven Stairway," that goes up the hill. By climbing this, visitors ultimately reach the Gate of Heaven; it is thought that as people rise higher above the earth, they get closer to heaven. Two gate buildings are located along the stairway and are designed hierarchically, in order to reflect their adjacency to the Ancestral Temple. The first gate building has the simplest form, featuring a single-pitched, gabled roof. The plan of the gate itself combines the forms of the circle and square in order to symbolize the combination of heaven and earth. The second gate building is larger than the first. The roof of this building is half-gabled and half-hipped. After passing through these gates, visitors arrive at a water pond that symbolizes the mythical water abyss that surrounds Mount Kunlun; it is thought that this mountain is the axis of the world and the pillar of heaven. The representation of the Kunlun Mountain in the temple complex consists of three parts: the mountain above the water, the water abyss itself, and the mountain under the water. The water is thought to be uncrossable by ordinary Daoists so a bridge, called "the Flying Bridge," spans the water pond and leads to the Gate of Heaven, the actual entrance to the temple.

The Ancestral Temple, like most of other Chinese buildings, consists of a roof; a middle body including columns and other structural elements, such as walls and partitions; and a terrace at the base. In designing the temple, we first had to choose a suitable style for the roof. For thousands of years roofs have developed, and they have become the most important feature of individual buildings and of groups of buildings. This is true of temple roofs as well. The roof can feature either single or double layers, with the latter being hierarchically more significant. Wutien, a four-pitched, single-layered style, was chosen for the Ancestral Temple. As the temple is located within a living community, the style of the roof is simpler than those found in the

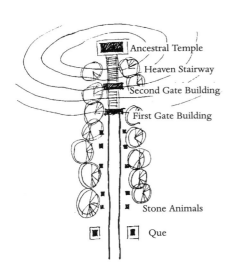

Site plan showing the location of the Village of Long Happiness's Spirit Road and Ancestral Temple.

Aerial view of the Village of Long Happiness's Ancestral Temple.

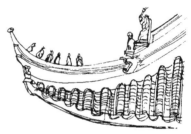

Village of Long Happiness, Ancestral Temple. View of flying swallow eave featuring Daoist immortals.

Village of Long Happiness, Ancestral Temple. View of flying swallow eave with fish symbolism.

imperial palaces of a larger district. The single Wutien style roof chosen for the Ancestral Temple, however, has the greatest hierarchy of any of the roofs within this community; the Wutien style can be used only in religious or imperial buildings.

In Western buildings, pitched roofs, seen from the side, tend to appear to be made up of simple triangles. The rafters of Chinese roofs, on the other hand, are not straight. They consist, instead, of many short sections that seem to cascade over the purlins like a long, gently breaking wave. This is done in order to avoid the triangular form that is thought by the Chinese to bring bad luck. As the eaves are greatly overhanging, the curve of the roof appears to be even more distinct, and this becomes the most important visual feature of the building as a whole. Further, short false eaves are employed at the very tips of the roof lines to intensify the beauty of the curve. These are called "flying swallow" eaves and are often decorated with terra-cotta figures representing dragons, and animals such as birds and dogs. Sometimes representations of Daoist immortal sages appear on flying swallow eaves too.

The end of the roof's ridge pole is also decorated with terra-cotta animal faces, often including combinations such as dragons and fish. The fish symbol on the top of the roof is believed to protect the wooden temple structure from fire. Water lilies are also used as a decorative subject. Like fish,

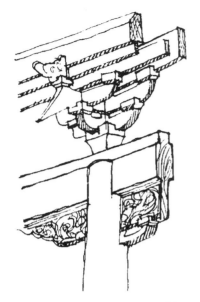

Post and lintel bracket used in the Village of Long Happiness's Ancestral Temple.

Dragon-encircled column in the Village of Long Happiness's Ancestral Temple.

water lilies are associated with water. The ridge pole itself is frequently decorated with alternating concave and convex tiles featuring abstract representations of bats. The word for bat, fu, is a homonym for happiness, although it is written as a different character. Because of this, the bat is a popular image for Chinese people who associate it with good fortune.

To support elaborate roofs of this type, a structural system containing post and lintel beams and brackets was developed by the Chinese. This system was applied to the design of the Ancestral Temple. The structural system is similar to today's post and beam construction—neither the exterior nor interior walls carry loads other than those of their own weight. The advantage of this system is that it facilitates the building of large, overhanging eaves that are supported by the brackets and lintels. The bracket system is a complicated modular arrangement of arms and stiffeners that are all mortised; not a single nail is used in the construction. The repetition of these bracket-arm modules also adds great beauty to the architecture—both interior and exterior. The bracket-arm modules rise from the columns, like branches from a tree trunk, to support the enormous weight of roof.

In general, the weight of the roof is carried down to the ground through the circular wooden columns. The columns are given different names according to their positions within a structure. The columns underneath the deep projecting eaves around the building are called "Eaves Columns," or "Yanzhu." In an important building such as an ancestral temple, two sets of surrounding "Yanzhu" columns can be used. The motif used to decorate the lintels and columns in such a case would be the dragon. Thus dragon-encircled columns are used in the Ancestral Temple to symbolize the spiral movement of the Dao.

The structural columns intersect with a terrace made of stone. Like the roof, the terrace is oversized and symbolically designed too. It has four stairways connecting the four directions of universe. Each of the stairways consists of nine steps to symbolize the nine levels of heaven. At the top of this hill where the Ancestral Temple stands, there is a water pond. This water pond is located at the summit of the mountain and is called "Yangtianchi," meaning "a lake that looks up to Heaven." This water pond is designed so that it becomes a "puff of breath permitting communication with the seat of god"—to quote a description from a poem written by the famous poet Li Bai.[4]

Historically, there were many different types of religious buildings in China due to the diversity of Chinese religions. Two of the principal kinds, however, were temples and monasteries. Daoist monasteries appeared much later than temples, however. Initially Daoists did not live together but rather isolated themselves from one another in the mountains. With the formal development of the religion, however, Daoists started to live together, and they built monasteries for this purpose.

Religious temples and monasteries were usually built to reflect the patterns of human beings' relationship with heaven. The Xuangong monastery in Shanxi, for example, was built along the cliff of a mountain. The name of the monastery expressed a metaphor for closeness to heaven, and the design embodied the Daoists' belief that the way to heaven was always difficult. As noted earlier, this theme of access to heaven was connected to the Daoist legend of Mount Kunlun. According to Daoism, Kunlun was the cardinal axis of the universe and the heaven pillar through which the divine forces from heaven came down to the earth and dispersed. More commonly, the metaphor of access to heaven was expressed in the architectural pattern of the Heaven Stairway. Several mountains in China had a Heaven Stairway: among them were Mount Tai, located in the east; Mount Hua, in the west; Mount Han, to the south; and Mount Song in the country's interior.

In the case of Mount Tai, the Gate of Heaven and the religious temples are located at the top. The only way to arrive there is to climb up thousands of "heaven stairs." At the summit of the sacred mountain of the west, Mount Hua, the "well of heaven" (Tien Jing) is located. The shaft was cut in order to permit the passage of only one person at a time. The cavity twists, and one climbs up by following the turnings to a height of more than fifty feet. On the mountain there is still a narrow thread of water that flows in the shaft, but without dampening it too much. All those who climb the mountain access it through the wall of heaven—there is no other route. At the Zhaogao monastery of Shanxi this theme was carried out differently; the builders produced a series of brick and stone buildings leading to the summit.

The planning of the monasteries in Sichuan and at other settlements in China, such as Erwangmiao and Yuanminggong, clearly reflect the incorporation of Daoist principles into design. Both monasteries were built on the southern slopes of mountains, to protect themselves from the malicious Qi that

View of Xuangong monastery in Shanxi.

View of the Heaven Stairway at Mount Tai.

comes from the north. The intricate and interesting roof shapes and utilitarian spaces were well blended with nature. The patterns of the Dragon Mountain and Tiger Mountain were not, however, naturally present in the landscape of the sites. To overcome this, armchair-shaped walls, which served as metaphors of the Dragon and Tiger mountains, were built to the north of the monasteries.

Other approaches were also used to promote beneficial Qi on the site of the monasteries. Jici, in the Shanxi province, for example, was designed in a garden style consistent with Daoist ideas of interactions between people and nature. The complex was built to the south of a group of mountains. Although the entire temple was asymmetrically laid out, there was an implied axis running from the complex's main entrance to the main shrine. An artificial water course meandered to the south of the monastery to keep Qi circulating smoothly. The water course carrying beneficial Qi flowed straight to the main temple building. A "Flying Bridge" was built above the water course right in front of the main building. Though this cross-shaped bridge itself was unique in Chinese architectural history, the idea of building a bridge in front of buildings was thousands of years old. Bridges are a symbol of beneficial Qi generation. They were sometimes built merely to serve as a lucky symbol, as was the case, for example, with a small arched-bridge at the foot of the first gateway entrance in the Nanshan monastery in the Shanxi province.

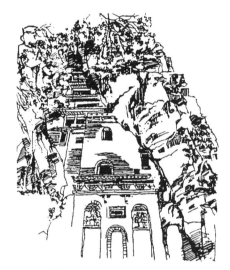

View of Zhaogao monastery at Shanxi.

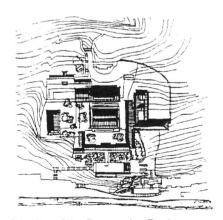

Site plan of the Erwangmiao Daoist monastery, Shanxi.

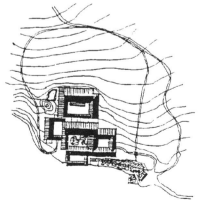

Site plan of the Yuanminggong Daoist monastery, Shanxi.

Perspective of Jici Daoist Temple in Shanxi.

Flying Bridge at Jici Temple, Shanxi.

TOMBS

Though not addressed in detail in the Village of Long Happiness, historically the design of tombs has been of great importance to the Chinese. Many of the architectural and decorative features found in town planning and in the design of religious structures are found in tombs as well. The Chinese saw an intrinsic continuity between the living and the dead. According to Chinese beliefs, the spirits of dead people gave them power over the fortunes, fate, and circumstances of the living. In the practice of Feng Shui a dwelling for the dead (Yinzhai) was considered to be just as important as a dwelling for the living (Yangzhai). The rules applied to Yinzhai and Yangzhai were interchangeable. One of the specific beliefs of the Daoist tradition of ancestral worship was that the souls of ancestors were linked with the sites of tombs. Among ancestors, emperors had the most significant effects on their decedents, as the emperor was considered to be the Son of Heaven and the Father of the Kingdom. Great attention was paid to the flow of Qi when imperial tombs were built.

First entrance gateway at Nanshan Monastery.

The tomb of the first Chinese emperor, Qinshihuang, was located in what is now the Shanxi province. The remains of the tomb consist of a human-made plot of rammed earth in the shape of a pyramid. The site for the tomb had very good features. To the south of the tomb were high mountains, which served as a defense, and to the north of the tomb was a wide plain, across which a tributary of the Wei River meandered. From the top of the tomb mountain one could see a great dis-

Que of the Qian Tomb, Tang dynasty.

Stele of the Qian Tomb, Tang dynasty.

tance. This tomb's site was, however, different from those described in Feng Shui's classic texts because of the use of different orientations. The ideal tomb site—that is, one that generates beneficial Qi—should generally be located to the south of large mountains, with the mountains to the north serving as a defense. This deviation from the norm was probably due to the fact that, during the Qin dynasty, the empire's enemies were located to the south of the empire so that the use of southern mountains as a defense might have seemed more appropriate.

The Ming Tombs (Shisanling), located in the suburbs of Beijing, provide a more typical example. The tomb area was surrounded by mountains on three directions: the north, east, and west. These mountains form a perfect armchair shape so that almost ideal Qi was generated. Each of the thirteen tombs is located on a mountain peak, with the first emperor of the Ming dynasty having the largest tomb. The entrance to the entire tomb complex consists of a memorial archway in stone. The axis that begins at the archway extends for eleven kilometers until it reaches the Tianshou Mountain, where the Chang Tomb was located.

The Qian tomb, where the emperor Tang Gaozong and the empress Wu Zetian were buried, was the biggest of all the imperial tombs of the Tang dynasty. The Qian tomb was built during the dynasty's prosperous period. The empress Wu Zetian was famous for her luxurious and sumptuous style of life. As a result, the Qian tomb includes many great projects such as the Bright Hall (Mingtang), the Heaven Temple, and other temples.

As noted earlier tombs, being the connection between heaven and earth, should incorporate both round and square visual concepts. A tomb that was excavated in Nanjing, for example, featured a design combining the square and circle in both plan and section. The plans of the tombs of all of the emperors of the Ming dynasty, such as Changling, also consisted of combinations of the square and the circle.

SYMBOLISM

Imperial tomb complexes were usually laid out symmetrically. The monumental sculptures of the Spirit Road were in pairs, and each pair of sculptures was placed on either side of the road, facing each other. The symbolic number two was associated with the balance of the Yin and Yang forces. The use of symbolism is an integral part of traditional Chinese architecture. Stone sculptures of animals, warriors, and officials have particular importance. These stone sculptures are believed to have the inherent power of the images they represent. According to the principles of Li, an image could bring about what it represented or symbolized. As Ann Paludan noted in her book *The Chinese Spirit Road:*

> The picture or stone relief of an ordered society would, for example, by its existence strengthen the society. The statue of a fierce beast would deter both human wrongdoers and evil spirits. This belief that an image would influence both the material and spiritual worlds applied to all kinds of images. In the case of stone, however, its effect was magnified through the association of stone with immortality. Stone endured, it possessed longevity, itself a means for attaining immortality. The powers of a stone figure were thus designed for eternity.[5]

Stone sculpture of a carp.

In Chinese architecture itself, symbolism of powerful subjects was reflected in many different patterns of sculpture, depiction, and decoration. As in the Spirit Road, stone sculptures of fierce animals were traditionally used as guards in front of the entrances to buildings and precincts. Carp were popular animal subjects because it was believed that they were able to swim upstream. Carp were symbolically used to combat evil Qi, which flowed downstream. In addition to carp, lions and dogs, which were thought to be strong, were often used images. The most popular animals for symbolic use, however, were the animals of the four quarters: the azure dragon, the white tiger, the red phoenix, and the black warriors (the turtle and snake). Depictions of these animals were usually placed in the direction that they were associated with. Tiles dating back to the Han dynasty (207 B.C. to A.D. 220) have been found that feature these four symbolic animals. Tiles featuring dragons were placed at the eastern edge of the roof, tiles of tigers were found at the western edge of the roof, those of the red phoenix were placed to the south, and tiles with images of the black warriors were placed on the northern side of the roof.

Tiles from the Han dynasty.

Sculpted detail of a railing in the Nanjing Friendship Garden at the Missouri Botanical Gardens, St. Louis, showing a stylized phoenix form. *(Photo: Jack Jennings, courtesy of the Missouri Botanical Gardens)*

Window in the shape of a peach, Summer Palace, Beijing.

Forms of stylization of the character "Shou," or "longevity."

The symbolic use of plants was just as popular as the use of animals. The most common trees used were the pine, banana, plum, peach, phoenix, and willow. Also popular were bamboo, chrysanthemums, peonies, lotuses, and orchids. Pine trees were symbolic of nobility and longevity; they grow from rocks, so pine trees and rocks were thought to share the same spirit. Also, aged pines are curved and gnarled, resembling a dragon dancing; therefore pine trees were most often incorporated with imperial architecture. In front of the imperial Hall of Benevolence and Longevity in Beijing, for example, miniature pines were placed. In addition, at the Altar of Heaven in Beijing, pine trees were planted. Peach trees were also assigned several symbolic meanings. Peach flowers, for example, symbolized new life, and the peach itself was thought to represent good health and immortality. The peach tree found on Mount Kunlun was said to bear fruit every 3,000 years; with one bite of these peaches, one could achieve eternal life. The peach as a symbol of longevity has long been used in buildings. A window in the Summer Palace in Beijing, for instance, was framed in the shape of a peach.

Another popular symbolic motif was the use of characters of the Chinese language. Many words, such as those for happiness and prosperity, could serve as decorative symbols for fortune or happiness. The most common of these was the character Wan that means "ten thousand" and that is written in the form of a Chinese swastika. The character of Shou, "long life," was also popular and was stylized in many different ways. Often the swastika motif was incorporated along with calligraphy. Shou, for example, is related to Wan—both mean "many." Xi means "joyful" or "happiness." If the character Xi was repeated twice, it meant "double happiness." Shuangxi, a symbol that was associated with weddings, was also frequently used and was thought to have an auspicious meaning.

The Chinese traditionally liked to use the symbols of objects that had names that were homophones with other words. The use of this type of symbolic motif was especially fashionable during the late Qing dynasty. As noted earlier, one of the commonest of these was the depiction of bats—fu—to represent happiness or luck. The character for fu, along with bats, was often used on the ridge of building roofs.

These various uses of symbolism could also be combined in a single architectural element. In a square window in a garden in Suzhou, for example, the window grilles were designed featuring representations of leaves, flowers, and tea pots, all within a Chinese swastika motif. On the ridges of roofs, different symbolic subjects could also be used. Decoration of the ridge pole could be connected with the theme of the swastika alone; with water plants and the swastika; with dragons and fishes; or with the water lily. The decorative motif of the ridge itself, however, most often featured representations of bats. As on the roof ridge, water plants and dragon or fish symbols were commonly used in the decoration of beams, columns, and on the joints of beams and columns. Just as individual subjects, such as dragons and fish, were thought to possess the power of the images they represented, the same was thought to be true of the depiction of scenes. In many Chinese religious structures, for example, stone stelae were carved that featured plans of the entire temple or monastery complex. These were believed to be powerful talismans that were able to protect the building that they were housed in.

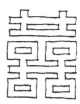

Forms of stylization of the character "Xi," or "happiness."

Square window in a garden wall, Suzhou.

Detail of the back wall in the Nanjing Friendship Garden at the Missouri Botanical Gardens, St. Louis, showing a plum flower opening and interlocking "fu" (bat) tiles across the top of the wall. *(Photo: Peggy Kelly, courtesy of the Missouri Botanical Gardens)*

Houses and commercial buildings

Of all the buildings within the Village of Long Happiness, the houses must respond to the greatest number of pragmatic constraints. As was the case with town planning, the design of religious structures, and as will be seen in the layout of the gardens, the forms of the houses are also governed by Daoist beliefs. In the section that follows, a series of patterns will be reviewed to demonstrate how philosophical ideas influenced the design of the houses within the village.

The main consideration in the design of housing was to maximize the flow of positive Qi and to eliminate any arrangements of space that might give rise to, or enhance, the presence of harmful Qi. The consideration of Qi in Chinese traditional dwellings was based on a simple principle: It was thought that the dwellings were themselves able to breath. Through openings, such as doors and windows, arrangements were made so that dwellings could inhale beneficial Qi and exhale harmful Qi. The location of houses on sites that had a potential for good Qi was very important.

Aerial view of the housing clusters in the Village of Long Happiness. The Winter cluster is to the north, Spring is in the east, Summer to the south, and Autumn in the west (the model is oriented to the north).

LOCATING HOUSES

As noted earlier, there are four housing clusters in the Village of Long Happiness, each named for the garden located within it. The location of individual houses within the clusters follows certain rules to help ensure that they are in harmony with the flow of Qi. Traditionally, Chinese houses are located on a grid pattern, with their entries to the south, opening onto a street running from east to west. The entrance will be set back from the street in order to leave some space for beneficial Qi, which is believed to be flowing by, to gather. If, on the other hand, a house is situated at the end of a long street, it is thought that the occupants will have bad luck because evil Qi can flow directly from the street into the house. Similarly, when a house is situated at the inner angle of Y-shaped streets, it is considered to have bad luck too because the central street runs toward the house like an arrow. (An arrow-shaped object is considered to have bad luck, and designers should avoid pointing such a shape toward a house.) On the other hand, when a house is built near a river, the entrance should face the direction of the flowing

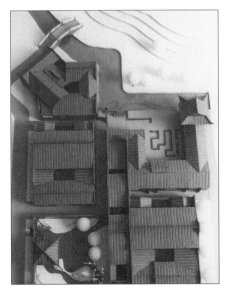

Aerial view of the Spring housing cluster in the Village of Long Happiness (model).

water and any bridges, in order to take advantage of the beneficial Qi that is thought to be borne by flowing water.

If a house or a community was not located to the south of an armchair-shaped mountain range, as is ideal, several methods could be used to enhance the vitality of the area's Qi. A grove of trees could be planted to the north of the site, for example, as was the case in a small community in Guangdong province. This armchair shape could be echoed in the form of the walls surrounding the house or in the layout of the rooms within the house. An example of the use of these principles is found in the Qi house of Yong'an in the Fujian province, a large rammed-earth dwelling that featured a central courtyard. The northern part of the house was built in an armchair shape, and when viewed in section, one can see the curves of the roofs that were created to simulate the landscape features of the Dragon and Tiger Mountains.

From the point of view of Qi, building a house near a meandering water course is always a wise choice. The entrance of the house should be oriented to face the direction in which water flows in order to maximize the amount of beneficial Qi that could be drawn into the house. An example of this can be seen in the Zhang house, a dwelling located in the town of Xinquan in the Fujian province. The entrance was altered so that it faced the direction of the flow of running water to, it

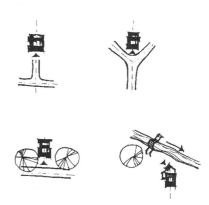

Diagrams of house entrance placement in relationship to flowing water and bridges.

View of a village in the Guangdong province.

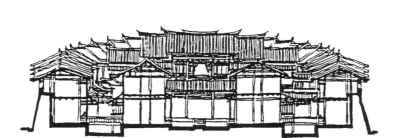

Section of Qi house, Yong'an.

Perspective of Qi house, Yong'an.

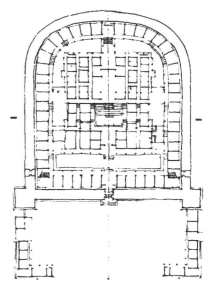

Plan of Qi house, Yong'an.

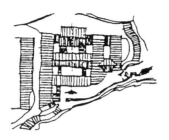

Plan of Zhang house, Xinquan, Fujian province.

Aerial view of a courtyard house (model).

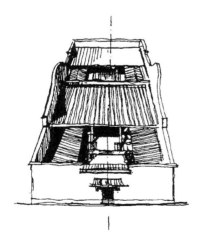

Aerial perspective of a typical courtyard house, showing axis.

was thought, allow luck and wealth to run directly into the house. The Lou house, of Liu Creek, had the same feature. In this case, however, more attention was paid to the bridge standing beside the house. This house also featured a private garden, and the side facing the river and the bridge was open. Two pavilions were built to "frame" the view of the bridge.

View of Zhang house, Xinquan, Fujian province.

STREET VIEW

The quality that the Chinese value most in their houses is seclusion. The more wealthy a family was traditionally, the deeper the house and the taller its walls. The house was thought to be a place of retreat, featuring complete privacy from the outside world. Families enjoyed the sun in secluded verandas and courtyards, where they experienced the harmonious rhythm and pulse of the universe.

People standing in the streets of the housing clusters would immediately notice the houses' tall exterior walls. Over the walls, the tops of trees could be indistinctly seen too. The view from the street is much more unified than those typically found in a Western neighborhood. The scene is not visually boring, however, as the walls themselves vary in texture and materials. The tall exterior walls, in addition to providing privacy, are used for fire protection. The main material for the houses themselves typically was wood, so the exterior walls were built of stone, earth, and other fire-retardant materials. In some cases, abstract symbols of animals and plants that are associated with water, such as fish and seaweed, were used as motifs for the decoration of the exterior walls.

COURTYARD HOUSE

As noted, the house is separated from the outside world by walls. The interior of the house, however, is designed in order to promote communication with heaven. The central feature of the houses is an interior courtyard, also called the "Heaven Well," that is surrounded by rooms in four directions. Usually, the courtyard is square in shape, following the square layout of the entire house (square is used in both cases to symbolize the earth). The courtyard is the place where families make sacrifices to heaven. The dimensions of the courtyard are dictated by the height of the rooms surrounding it. This, in turn, determines the quality of light from the sky that it receives. The designer's aim is to ensure that when the family members are sitting in the courtyard, they can look up over the low roof and have an unobstructed view of the sky. At the southeast corner of the courtyard a central drainage pit is located in order to symbolize the water abyss of the earth that, according to Daoist teachings, is believed to be located in the southeast corner of the earth.

Aerial view of housing (model).

SYMMETRICAL LAYOUT

Each house in the village has a symmetrical axis that begins at the southern entrance and runs to the northern back door of the house. The different functional spaces are arranged in relationship to this axis. The sequence of spaces, starting from the south, is front porch; main entrance gates (single or double); entrance hall; miniature gardens (usually placed against a shadow wall); shadow wall; courtyard; hall holding the altar table; the altar table itself; the interior partition wall against which the altar table is placed; and, finally, the back courtyard and its exit door. If the house does not have a shadow wall to prevent the flow of evil Qi, the entrance and the exit cannot both be on the same axis. This will prevent evil Qi from going through the house to the family altar place, which is very inauspicious.

Traditional Chinese houses have only a small front porch, most often with a set back gate. As most Chinese houses are built along a street that runs from east to west, a little set back space is required to be able to retain the beneficial Qi that is flowing down the street. Front porches typically feature a small curved roof and few stairs. A pair of stone animal sculptures will often be put in front of the porch steps. As on the Spirit

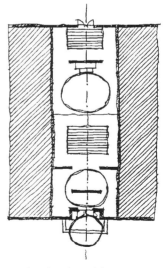

Diagram showing the axial arrangement of a courtyard house.

View of entryway with lion sculptures.

View of decorated front doors.

View of the shadow wall in the entry hall.

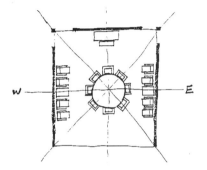

Plan of central hall.

Road, the images of stone animals are thought to be living protectors of the house. As these animals play the role of guardians of fortune, lions are the only appropriate choice.

Continuing through the front porch, one would face a pair of exterior doors that serve as the house's "front gate." The door panels are decorated with nails and copper door knobs to form a representation of a tiger's face. If the door itself is not decorated with animal symbols to prevent the entry of evil Qi, at least a pair of auspicious couplets, written on red paper, will be placed on the door panel in order to bring the house good luck. The color red is used because it is associated with the southerly orientation of the front gate. If, however, someone has died in the house, the couplets will be written on white paper.

There are two halls on the house's main axis: the entrance hall and the large central hall. Upon entering the doors to the house, one will be in the small entrance hall with plain guest chairs. The furniture is simply designed as this place is intended for very short term waiting. This entrance hall is half open to the courtyard but separated by a shadow wall. The shadow wall will be specially designed to prevent the flow of evil Qi and to attract beneficial Qi. The forms of the square and circle are used here as symbols of communication with the universe. Miniature plants will be put in front of the shadow wall. (One Daoist meditation technique consists of gazing at miniature gardens in order to cultivate good Qi.)

After going around the shadow wall, visitors arrive at the central courtyard. Facing the courtyard on the north side is the main building of the house—a tall hall containing the family's altar table. This hall will be taller than the buildings to its side, but it can still be only one story in height. The hall itself will house multiple functions. In addition to being a place of worship, it can also be a living room for the entire family to gather. Special entertainment, such as the celebration of seasonal festivals, will take place here.

In the central hall, where the ancestral altar is placed, the furniture should be very formal. It will be symmetrically arranged in a square space, consistent with the square house and square earth. In the center of this square a round table is placed for use during family occasions. There are usually eight seats placed around such tables to symbolize the eight cosmological directions. The head of the family will sit in a chair to the north of the table, facing the south.

The hall is a focus of decoration—on structural elements, such as columns, beams, brackets, and lintels, as well as on the nonstructural interior walls. Decorative brackets, for example, will be used under the eaves of the hall. At the back of this hall, the family altar table is positioned against a full-height wall featuring very elaborate decorations. The altar table is usually tall and long. An incense burner and a miniature landscape are often put on the table. Altars generally feature a miniature landscape whose subject is the Three Isles of the Blessed—the places where the Daoist immortal sages are thought to live.

If visitors continue around and past the altar table, they will return to the axis, on which a small back service yard is located. On the axis, a very simple door will connect the backyard to the outside world. The door will open outward to be consistent with the direction of flowing Qi.

Historically, the flow of Qi has also been the focus of house design. In the case of a courtyard house in Beijing, Qi was well directed. In this case, however, the entrance to the central courtyard was not on the central axis. Instead, it was offset in order to prevent the direct flow of Qi into the courtyard, which would be a negative force in the household. This type of entrance location could also be found in houses in other regions where the climate and the landscape were quite different. In the Guangdong province, for example, where the weather was usually very hot, courtyards were built as small as possible in order to reduce heat gain from the sun. The houses were also less deep in order to increase ventilation in the north-south direction. In the case of a residence in Suzhou, the main entrance was located on the central axis of the house, but the inner entrance was not located on center in order to prevent Qi

"Three Isles of the Blessed" miniature landscape.

Inner screen of a courtyard house, Beijing.

Main courtyard of a courtyard house, Beijing.

Inner entrance of a courtyard house, Beijing.

Aerial view of a courtyard house, Beijing.

View of a courtyard house in the Fujian province.

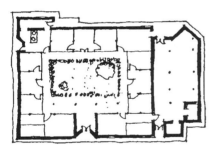

View of a courtyard house in the country-side

from coming straight into the house. In this house a shadow wall was placed in front of the main hall in order to ward off evil Qi. To further slow the flow of Qi, the exit of the house was not placed on the central axis either.

The Chinese principle of balancing Yin and Yang forces was deeply embedded in the patterns of Chinese living space. As demonstrated, the plans of Chinese houses in various regions and environmental settings were basically square in shape and featured central courtyards. These courtyards were often given a somewhat unearthly feeling through the inclusion of miniature plants. Within Chinese houses, curves and winding geometrical lines were considered to be beneficial ways of redirecting straight flowing, harmful Qi. As demonstrated in the Huan house in the Fujian province, these streamlined walls can be a house's most attractive feature.

View of roof of Huan house, Fujian province.

View of Huan house, Fujian province.

SPACE PLANNING AND INTERIOR ARRANGEMENT

In Chinese houses rooms are arranged around a central axis. These rooms typically include bedrooms, a study room, a guest room, a kitchen, washroom, and storage. Since the entire house is square in order to reflect the shape of the earth, each room in the house will likewise be located to reflect its meaning in Chinese cosmology.

Domestic life in China was strongly bound to the earth, and to the Yin force. The numbers used symbolically in domestic life were, therefore, mostly even ones. In a typical plan of a Chinese house, there was an even number of rooms. Within a room, there was usually an even number of pieces of furniture too. Square tables, hexagonal tables, and octagonal tables were popular. There was an even number of cabinets placed in spaces, within which there was an even number of drawers.

Bedrooms

The hierarchy of the family is also mirrored in the arrangement of the rooms, with the most important spaces being the bedrooms. The relative importance of these, from highest to lowest in the family hierarchy, are the grandparents' bedroom, the parents' bedroom, and the children's bedroom. All of these rooms will be located near the central hall. The grandparents' bedroom is located to the east of the central hall. The rising sun from the east is said to be a good omen for older people. Living with one's aged parents is the traditional custom in China, and elderly people are highly valued members of society. The parents' bedroom is located to the west of the central hall, and the children's bedroom will be on this same side.

In the bedrooms, the first concern is to establish the location of the bed. Beds are usually placed so that the sleeper's head will be to the east and his or her feet will be to the west. The human body is thought to be a microcosm of the universe as a whole; the center of the head and the belly are called "Kunlun" in Chinese, a reference to the mountain that is believed to be the center of the universe. The beds chosen for the rooms are oversized, painted red, and decorated with flowers and birds. If a visitor enters a Chinese bedroom, he or she should not be able to see the sleeper's feet. It is also important that only a few other pieces of furniture be present in the bedroom, such as a dresser and a dressing table. A sitting place can be arranged

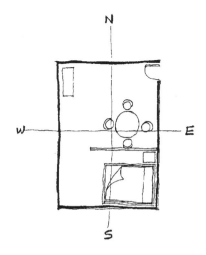

Plan of a typical bedroom.

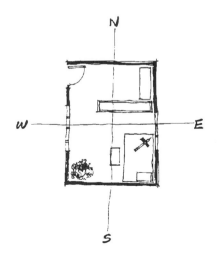

Plan of a scholar's study.

within the bedroom, but if this is done, a screen will be used to separate the sitting area and the sleeping area. This screen can be either of latticework, to enhance the transparent beauty of the space, or it can consist of an entire decorated panel.

Study

A study is a very important room in a scholar's family. It is placed some distance from the living area for maximum seclusion. A study facing a courtyard that is open to the sky is especially good. In the courtyard itself trees or a miniature garden will be planted. The growth of the plants symbolizes the increase of knowledge. The study room will also have a window facing east, a direction that is associated with the rising sun. On a typical day a scholar might get up early in the morning and begin her day with some meditation by gazing at the miniature gardens in the courtyard. In this way she can cultivate her own positive Qi by "tapping into" the flow of cosmic Qi that is directed into the Heaven Well. On other days she might read a book while wandering through the miniature gardens, deep in thought about the fundamental nature of the Daoist world. After finishing some philosophical readings, she could open the eastern window to feel the rays of the early morning sun.

Normally, the study room should be very spacious. No furniture other than the scholar's table, a chair, a bookcase, and a low table on which to place a musical instrument is found in the study room. Traditionally a Chinese scholar was able to write, paint, do calligraphy, and play music. This study room might be called a "Zhai," which means "a place of fasting" in both Daoism and Buddhism. It is very important for the scholar to have a big table on which she can lay her paintings and rolls of calligraphy. Chinese brush painting requires only a horizontal working surface. On the table itself, the scholar might display her Four Precious Things of Study: an inkwell, inkstone, brush, and brush holder. The inkwell will be a piece of rock carved in the shape of the Three Isles of the Blessed. In spite of its small size, the Three Isles of the Blessed inkwell will represent, to Daoists, a place of retreat.

shān

Above: *View of Xuangong monastery,*
Shanxi province.

city

石

Guest room

The guest room will be placed outside the realm of the family's life. Though distance is required from the family's bedrooms, a guest is still very important to the family. A room near the entrance is most appropriate.

Kitchen

To the Chinese, cooking is so important an activity that a special altar is set up in the kitchen for the "God of the Stove," who blesses the health and wealth of the family. A picture of this household god is put on the wall of the kitchen, and it will be replaced at the beginning of every new year when the God of the Stove returns to heaven to report on the behavior of the family over the course of the past year. The kitchen is also important in Chinese culture because it is the place where the hearth is located. According to traditional Chinese beliefs, the hearth is thought to be open to the sky, and to heaven. The hearth symbolizes the pillar of heaven and the axis of the universe—Mount Kunlun—as well as the exchanging of Yin and Yang forces between earth and heaven. The actual pillar of heaven is believed to be situated at the northeast corner of the earth, so the kitchen is located in that corner of the house.

The kitchen is an important place not only due to its association with its special god but also because of the significance of its interior elements. The five elements—earth stove, wood fuel, burning fuel, metal wok, and water boiling in the wok—have a very special meaning to the Chinese. They complete the cycle of Five Elements—the universal flow of earth, wood, fire, metal, and water. According to Daoist teachings, the Five Elements are believed to combine to create the world. Traditionally the Chinese gave a great deal of attention to the arrangement of the Five Elements within the kitchen to ensure that the elements would not come into contact and thereby destroy one another. For example, the sink and the stove cannot be put in the same counter, as in some American kitchens, because fire and water destroy one another, which would prevent the completion of the circle of the Five Elements.

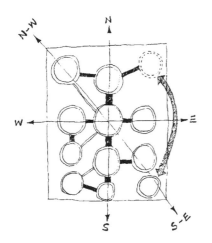

Diagram showing the "adjustment" made to the washroom's placement.

Washroom

The washroom is considered to be the least important room in the house. Traditionally, washrooms are located outside the main structure. The washroom's drainage pit is thought to symbolize the drainage pit of the universe, which is located in the southwest corner of the earth. This arrangement, however, would result in the washroom being at the front of the house, which would be an unpopular choice. In our design, therefore, we decided to move the washroom to the northeast corner. It is, however, separated from the kitchen by the back service yard.

STRUCTURAL SYSTEM

The traditional Chinese post and lintel system of wood frame construction is used in the houses in the Village of Long Happiness, as it was in the Ancestral Temple. The roofs will be curved, featuring either a single or double pitch. The exterior walls are both load bearing and protective. They are made from earth, stone, and brick. Interior walls are non-load-bearing, and they are typically made of wood. Brackets on columns are used only under the roof of the main hall, and they have solely a decorative function.

The roofs of the main halls must be carefully designed; they will be curved and double-pitched. The ridge poles can be deco-

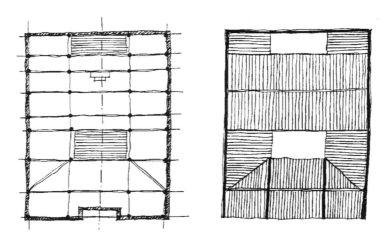

Diagrammatic representation of roof structure, with roof plan.

rated with convex and concave tiles featuring an abstracted representation of bats, which symbolize happiness. At the two ends of the ridge pole, only the figures of abstracted domestic animals, such as birds or the Chinese symbol of longevity, can be used.

This system of timber structure has been utilized in Chinese architecture for at least 3,000 years. In a site excavated in Xizhuangzhen, dating from the Han dynasty (207 B.C. to A.D. 220), evidence was found of the same basic form of Chinese timber structure used today. The first official record of timber structure, however, occurred during the Song dynasty (A.D. 1100), and it appeared in a book titled *Yingzao fashi*[6] that was compiled by Li Jie. Timber construction was termed "Big Wood Work" when used in palaces, temples, residences and "Small Wood Work" when architectural elements and furniture were built according the modular system.

View of the courtyard of the "handkerchief house," Fujian province.

NARROW HOUSES

Though most Chinese dwellings were close to square in plan, there were a few exceptions. One of the main reasons for varying the form was due to special physical characteristics of the site. In Quanzhou of the Fujian province, for example, a dwelling was built on an especially narrow site owing to the fact that the house was located in a busy commercial street where land was very expensive. The house was long and narrow and was called the "handkerchief house" by the local people. The length of the house provided seclusion, one of the primary qualities sought by most Chinese when building a house. Usually, the deeper a house is, the more courtyards it will contain. As depth is the primary quality sought by the Chinese, successful houses can readily be built on a very narrow strip of land.

In some cases, a large family might construct a number of these types of long strip houses side by side, with each single strip serving as a retreat for a subfamily. When poorer families cannot afford a broad site on which to build their house but still want secluded living, the solution is often a long and narrow house. This situation was addressed in the Village of Long Happiness in the Spring Housing Cluster houses, which were designed to combine the domestic and the commercial. The axis of the houses still runs from the south to the north, begin-

Aerial view of narrow houses in the Village of Long Happiness *(model)*.

ning with an entrance, first courtyard, ancestral hall, second courtyard, bedrooms, third courtyard, washroom and kitchen, fourth courtyard, and a private store, to be run by members of the family. There are also some instances in which a store might be located on the southern side of the house, facing the street.

HOUSES NEAR A BRIDGE

If there is a bridge near the house, the entrance should be altered so that it can open to the bridge and face the direction of the flowing river. In this kind of house the distinguishing central axis can be broken. There is still a main axis that leads people from the entrance to the courtyard, but the courtyard itself is no longer square in shape. From here, the axis shifts to the south-north orientation again. Continuing on along it, a visitor to the house would reach the altar table and the central hall.

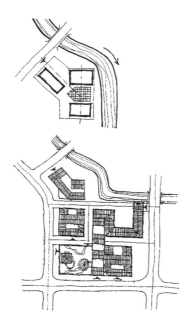

Plan showing entry locations for houses in relationship to orientation, the flow of water, and bridges.

View of entryway of a house facing a bridge (model).

COMMERCIAL PLACES

In China traditionally, commercial places were close to dwellings. As noted above, in some dwellings private shops are combined with houses. In the layout of a solely commercial place, however, the square grid pattern is again used. All the facades of the stores will face a square in the center, except for the ones that are located directly on the street. The northern side of the commercial square in the Village of Long Happiness is, however, open to provide a view of the river flowing by. There will be a tea house (on the second story), a restaurant, hair salon, and a grocery store. The tea house and the grocery are the most frequented of the commercial places, so they are placed by the side of the street. The main gate to the commercial area itself is located below the tea house.

View of commericial area entry, with tea house above *(model)*.

NINE TURN WATER COURSE

At the center of the commercial area, a meandering water course, based on traditional Chinese customs, is found. This winding water course will have nine turns to symbolize the nine turns of the Huang River, the main water course in Chinese geography. The nine turn water course is also believed to lead to Mount Kunlun—the central pillar of the universe. This winding water course is designed so that people can float their wine cups on it during the spring festival. The wine cups symbolize the comfort of family life, and they are floated in order to attract the lost souls of ancestors of the family. It is believed that after long travels among the souls of the dead, ancestors, thus summoned, will finally return to their home and family.

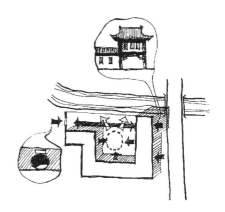

Diagram showing view of water from the commercial area.

Aerial view of the nine turn water course *(model)*.

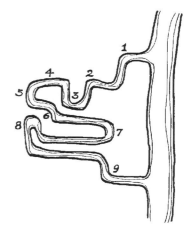

Diagram of the nine turn water course.

Gardens

Perhaps the most well known type of Chinese design, at least in the West, is the garden. Here, stripped of many of the functional requirements that must, of necessity, be addressed at other design scales, the manifestation of Chinese philosophical beliefs in built form can most clearly be seen. The principles used in traditional Chinese gardens are in contrast to those used in house. The symmetrical, square layout of houses suggested that people were rooted to the earth, whereas the asymmetrical gardens were regarded as a place of refuge from worldly concerns. The layout of the garden also symbolically embodied the movement of Five Elements, from the beginning of life in spring through the course of the seasons, cyclically.

Historically, most Chinese gardens were built in city or town environments, often as part of a dwelling. The gardens were intended as human-made landscapes where one could withdraw from ordinary, earthly life. The patterns of an ideal site according to the principles of Feng Shui were reduced to much smaller scales and incorporated into garden design. For instance, the idea of Dragon and Tiger mountain ranges were reduced to rocky hills, rocks, or rocks in containers in the garden. The ideal water course of Feng Shui was reduced to a small stream or to water ponds of different sizes. It was not necessary for these miniature mountain and water landscapes to be identical to the forms specified in Feng Shui texts. Rather, they were included in the garden as a kind of metaphorical "magnet" for magic, owing to the good geomantic influence they were thought to have and by their simulation of the abodes of the Daoist immortals. Building rocky hills in the center of a water pond became a popular style of garden design as it was believed that this attracted positive Qi.

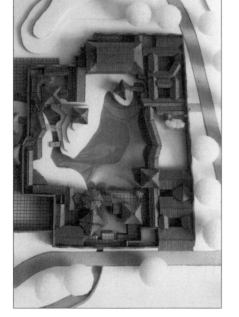

Aerial view of the Garden of Delight *(model)*.

CHOOSING GARDEN SITES

The first thing to be considered in building a garden is the choice of site. In the case of the Village of Long Happiness, the main garden in the town, the Garden of Delight, is located to the east. Unlike the relatively pragmatic housing clusters, gardens are more analogous to artistic creations, such as poems and paintings, though they exist in three dimensions. There are, of course, general rules to be followed, but the application of these principles is more flexible in gardens than in houses.

Water and mountains are two necessary elements within gardens. The height of the "mountain" or the depth of the water are not, however, particularly important. As Liu Yuxi wrote in the "Loushi Ming," "The miracle of a mountain is not that it is tall, but because it is the place where the immortals live; the charm of water is not that it is deep but because it carries dragon Qi."[7]

The Garden of Delight is built around an artificial lake, formed in the shape of a hand playing a flute. This represents the ideal Feng Shui form of a "Dragon Water Course." The beautiful landscape surrounding the lake is the focal point of the garden. An artificial peninsula has been built at the northern end of the lake; this peninsula is an abstract representation of Mount Kunlun, where the Daoist immortals are thought to live.

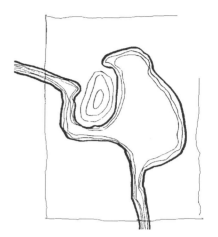

Site plan diagram showing the Dragon Water Course.

CIRCULATION ROUTE

There is a path laid out by which people may circulate through the garden. Visitors follow this specially designed route to best enjoy the scenery. Like a piece of music, the touring route has a prologue, a theme, a climax, and, upon return to the starting place, an epilogue. The entrance to the Garden of Delight is located at the southeast corner of the site. Upon entering the

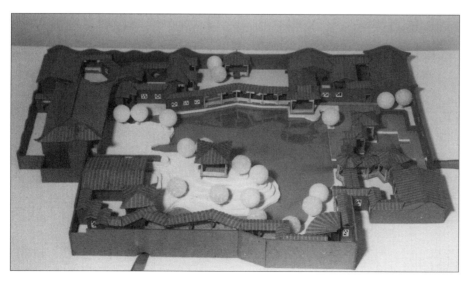

Overview of the Garden of Delight *(model)*.

View of the Courtyard of the Well in the Garden of Delight.

View of the Pavilion of the Gentle Breeze in the Garden of Delight.

garden, visitors arrive at the "Courtyard of the Well." This is a very small enclosed space surrounded by buildings on four sides. A person's view in this space is very constrained, as if he or she were sitting at the bottom of a well. This courtyard is characterized by quietness, and visitors do not linger here too long. This space serves only as a prologue for the spatial sequence to follow.

After passing several enclosed and semienclosed spaces, one arrives at the "Pavilion of the Gentle Breeze." From this pavilion, visitors can see the glimmer of ripples on the lake and feel the refreshing breeze coming from it. The contrast between the openness of the view of the lake and those of the smaller, enclosed courtyard spaces is vivid and is intended to create interest.

Visitors then go through the "Entering Picture" archway. The archway is open on two sides, with one opening facing the lake and the other looking onto a courtyard. This courtyard, which features a pavilion-like building, named "Semi-red and Semi-green," is dotted with many rocks, plants, and flowers. After exiting this space, visitors arrive at another group of courtyard garden buildings. This group, however, is quite different from those at the entrance. The archways here are interlocked, and the courtyards are linked to each other. The nature of the scenes changes quickly, and the flow of space is intentionally ambiguous.

View from the Entering Picture archway in the Garden of Delight.

View of grouped courtyard buildings in the Garden of Delight.

Visitors to the garden arrive next at a big hall. This is the main building in the garden and is called the "Chamber of Delight." It serves as the climax of the sequence of spaces in the garden. The hall is open to the lake and stands behind the peninsula. From the front of the hall, a view of the whole lake appears. To better enjoy the scenery of the garden, visitors can climb up to the second floor of the Chamber of Delight, where an elegant tea house is located. From this point, a view of the entire garden can be taken in.

Though the Chamber of Delight is the climax of the spatial sequence, the garden also has an epilogue. A wall standing outside of the "Gazing onto the Mountain" archway suggests to people that something is concealed behind it. From here it takes just a few steps to reach a Moon Gate called "Hidden Fragrance." This gate leads people to pass through the wall and arrive at a garden hall where plants flower during all four seasons—this is the place that houses the hidden fragrances. At the back of this hall, in the northwest corner of the garden, a small, quiet courtyard is located.

The western part of garden is slightly higher in elevation than the eastern part. Here there is a long zigzag arcade following a winding water course whose bank is dotted by rocks in a variety of shapes. The arcade itself is open to the lake. At the end of this archway there is a fan-shaped pavilion. This building stands at the southwest corner of the garden facing the main hall and entrance courtyard. Past this fan-shaped pavilion, an open archway spans an inner water pond, thus leading visitors to the last pavilion in the garden. A small gate serves as the garden's exit.

Historically, the gates of gardens were very important design features because they were the boundaries between the worldly and the "other-worldly." Gate designs used many different motifs. Gourd-shaped gates, like those used in Beijing, symbolized the Daoist notion of gardens being "another world." A moon-shaped gate in Wangsiyuan, featuring the inscription "Cloud Cave," incorporated rocks in its design to enhance the ethereal feeling of the garden. The most popular shape used in the gates of gardens was the circle. The view from a fan-shaped pavilion in the Summer Palace of Beijing, for example, was framed by a moon gate. There, the reflection of a semicircular arched bridge in the water is used visually to create a complete circle. Other shapes, such as vases, leafs, and other curvilinear forms, can also be used for gates.

View of the Garden of Delight, showing the Chamber of Delight (model).

View of the Garden of Delight's Hidden Fragrance Moon Gate.

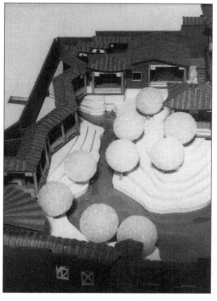

View of the winding arcade in the Garden of Delight (model).

View of the Garden of Delight's small exit gate.

Gourd-shaped gate in a garden, Beijing.

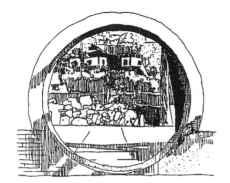

Moon Gate in the garden of the Summer Palace, Beijing.

The garden as a whole was thought to represent the universe in microcosm. The Chinese symbolism for the formal universe was, therefore, a recurrent theme in gardens. Polar opposites are presented throughout, such as the balance of Yin and Yang, solid and void, and so on. Gardens were designed so that the qualities that were absent were implied by those that were present. In a garden in Liuyuan, for example, a strong visual impact was created by door grilles and window panels that contrasted with the dark eaves above them. In the same garden, a dark, winding covered walkway contrasted with a lighter courtyard—the so called "entwined ancient tree courtyard." In this same garden, from the lake looking toward the walkway, the contrast between the picture window grilles and the white-washed wall suggested an oscillation between solidity and voidness, and between the monochromatic and the colorful.

In a well-known passage, the eighteenth century writer Shen Fu described the relationship of aesthetic motivation to symbolism in the Chinese garden:

In laying out garden pavilions and towers, suites of rooms and covered-walkways, piling up rocks in mountains, or planting flowers to form a desired shape, the aim is to see the small in the large, to see the large in the small, to see the real in the illusory and to see the illusory in the real.[8]

Ancient tree courtyard, Liuyuan, Suzhou.

Cloud Cave Moon Gate, Wangshiyuan, Suzhou.

Covered walkway in Liuyuan, Suzhou.

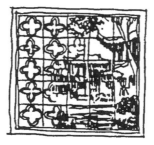

Window grille cover in the garden in Liuyuan, Suzhou.

Windows and doors with grille treatments, Liuiyuan, Suzhou.

View from a moon gate looking toward a pavilion in the Nanjing Friendship Garden at the Missouri Botanical Gardens, St. Louis, Missouri. *(Photo: Jack Jennings, courtesy Missouri Botanical Gardens)*

ROCKS AND WATER

In the Garden of Delight, artificial rocks and rock hills are located throughout the garden. The use of rocks in the garden evokes their use in Chinese paintings and poems. The rocks and rock hills are called "artificial" because they are in fact human-made, though an effort is made to assemble a natural-looking landscape. In making artificial rock arrangements, the designer seeks a balance of Yin and Yang forces and of solid and void. Three words are used to describe the art of making artificial rocks—Tou, Lou, and Shou. "Tou" means "penetration" or "communication," so these rocks have cavities throughout them. "Lou" rocks let water fall drop by drop through a hole at the top, but not too quickly. "Shou" means "sparseness," so these rocks should stand alone and upright. In addition, the top of them should be bigger than the bottom, so it looks as though the rock is able to fly. Though these three words seem to address only the void in the rocks, in actuality they address the relationship of voidness to solidity.

In a small garden courtyard, rocks are erected against white walls. The white wall becomes the metaphorical paper for the painting, and the rocks become the painting's subject. By looking through a window, the feeling of enjoyment of a "painting of rocks" is enhanced even further. A case such as this is found to the rear of the main garden hall, the Chamber of Delight, where delicate rocks are arranged against the northern wall.

Rocks in a small courtyard are usually arranged sparsely. In a large open space, however, rock hills can be built to give people the feeling of naturally occurring rock mountains. Rocky hills can also be used to separate open space; the shape of rocks used in this way is organic and amorphous. Like the rocky hills on the peninsula, these hills separate the space into two distinct areas—a northeast part and a northwest part—and they provide an organic connection between them.

Like the shadow wall in a dwelling, rocks can be used as an obstacle to obscure views and to prevent evil Qi from penetrating the inner garden, the place of Daoist retreat. In the Garden of Delight, rocks are placed in the courtyard behind the entrance hall, thus limiting one's view of the inner courtyard's garden. This lends the space an ambiguous, mystical quality.

Rocks are not only arranged on the land, they can also be placed in water courses. This kind of water course is sometimes called a "rocky pond," as the rock-covered bank serves to connect the land and water surface. The arrangement

Cloud-Capped Peak rock, the central focal point in the garden at Liuyuan, Suzhou.

of a rock bank should follow the rules of nature, being both winding and irregular. The presence of these irregularly shaped rocks also gives the water course a natural look. A calm water surface will reflect the shadows of rocks, thus enhancing their beauty. Rock symbolizes strength; water represents softness. This play of water and rock is another example of the balance of non-being and being that is central to Daoist thought.

Water in the garden is as important as rock. It provides charm and variety. Water is to the universe what blood is to a human body. In the Garden of Delight, the water pond dominates the entire space. It "borrows" the sky, thus making the garden seem larger than it is. It adds light by day and reflects the moon at night. The horizontal surface of the water contrasts with the verticality of the rocky mountains and garden buildings. There are both large and small bodies of water in the garden. The larger body is open and wide in order to accumulate positive dragon Qi. The smaller area is narrow and winding to inhibit the straight flow of evil Qi. The art of arranging water courses in gardens requires the careful balancing of Yin and Yang forces.

Rocks, and their reflections, in the garden at Liuyuan, Suzhou.

Historically, the interplay of rocks and water was also an important consideration in garden design. There are many examples that show how rocky hills and water ponds are present in gardens and are combined with garden architecture. An example of this occurs in the Imperial Garden in Beijing where longer ornamental rocks are placed in front of a pavilion. Similarly, in the central ambulatory space of Liuyuan, artificially placed rocks dominate the entire space. The "Cloud-Capped Peak," a piece of Tai Hu eroded limestone that rises to a height of twenty feet, was located beside a water pond in a garden in Liuyuan. In front of main hall of the garden, "The Winding Brook Building" (Quxilou), rocks and bodies of water are incorporated to provide the most auspicious visual effect. And in Zhanyuan of Nanjing, huge piles of rocky hills were built in the middle of a water pond to mimic the place where the immortals were believed to live.

View of rocks in the Zhanyuan garden, Nanjing.

PLANTS

All of the plants in the garden are thought to contain spirits that guide their destinies. In Chinese opera and theater these spirits take on human form and participate in adventures in the world of mortals. The plants used in the garden are the same as those depicted in Chinese artwork. In gardens, the artistic concepts used, for the most part, are connected with plants. In the "Listen to Falling Rain" archway, for example, banana trees become the main focus of the design. Plants serve as an intermediary between the changing nature of the weather and seasons, and their effect on people's feelings.

The most popular plants used in gardens include evergreens; conifers, such as pine trees; herbaceous trees, especially bamboo and banana; flowering trees, including plum and peach trees; flowers, notably chrysanthemums, peonies, lotuses, and orchids; and deciduous trees, like willows and the phoenix tree. The symbolic meanings associated with these plants were well understood by the Chinese.

As noted earlier, pine trees are symbolic of nobility and longevity. Because they grow from rock, pine trees and rocks are thought to share the same essential qualities. Aged pines are curved and gnarled and resemble a dragon dancing. Like pine trees, bamboo has many symbolic associations. Unlike other plants, however, bamboo plants have hollow central cores. Daoists, therefore, use bamboo to symbolize the free flow of Qi that circulates inside people's bodies. In addition, because bamboo doesn't blossom in the spring and compete with other

Views showing the placement of an individual tree within a courtyard.

flowers, they are associated with modesty. Banana trees are planted in the garden largely because of the delightful sound they produce when nature touches them—for example, when rain drops on their large oar-like leaves or when wind passes through them. To the Chinese these sounds are like those of a weeping girl. Plum trees are planted for the "plum blossoms," which are called "meihua" in Chinese. In the spring the meihua blossoms before any other plant. Though they look fragile, they are in fact able to withstand the cold wind of the earliest spring. These plum blossoms are also associated with longevity and rebirth. The other tree that is frequently used in the garden, and which produces flowers, is the peach tree. The peach flower symbolizes new life, and the peach fruit symbolizes good health and immortality. Peach flowers and plum flowers are often grouped together in a vase as a metaphor for friendship.

Deciduous trees are not as important as bamboos or pines, but they cannot be eliminated from the garden. The most popular of this type of tree are the willow and the phoenix. Willows symbolize feminine grace and are frequently planted beside the water. Phoenix trees have large leaves and green bark, which are thought to attract the descent of the magical phoenix bird to the site where they are planted.

The chrysanthemum is highly valued in China because it blossoms in late autumn. Because it "braves the frost," it is accorded respect like that given to the noble pine. The peony is the "King of Flowers" in China. Because the petals of the peony resemble a handful of Chinese coins, it symbolizes wealth. The lotus is also very popular in the garden. The lotus plant is remarkable in that all its parts can be used for medicine or food. The lotus is also associated with purity because it grows out of mud and yet is not defiled. Orchids are valued for the elegant beauty of their stripe-like leaves. The graceful essence of the plant can be represented with just one stroke of an artist's brush.

The arrangement of plants should be made according to the rules of balance between the plants themselves and the buildings that surround them. It is important to plant a single tall deciduous tree in one of the corners of the courtyard. The quality of the "void" space within the courtyard is determined by the placement of the tree planted in the corner. In larger courtyards, a single tree is not sufficient. In these cases, two or three deciduous trees should be planted. Attention should be paid in this case to ensure a balanced, asymmetrical arrange-

View of a banana tree from the Listen to the Falling Rain archway in the Garden of Delight.

Views showing the placement of a group of trees within a courtyard.

View of thickly planted trees in the garden.

ment. In even larger courtyards, the balance between a mass of trees, and their colors, should also be considered. In these cases, both deciduous trees and herbaceous trees are chosen so that the garden will be green through the four seasons. By thickly planting trees in the garden, a boundary layer can be created. The leaves and branches of these trees form a rhythm of sparseness and density, and of solidity and voidness. Looking through such plantings, one gets an impression of a deep, but indistinct, scenery that is highly valued by the Chinese. This tree boundary can define the space in much the same way as a rocky mountain does. It can also provide a background for other plants, especially in places where the boundary of the architecture is unclear.

View of a typical pavilion facade.

APARTMENTS AND PAVILIONS

The main hall of the Chamber of Delight is called a "Lou," or apartment. Originally, gardens were built for private living and entertaining, and the Lou itself was the place where the members of the family lived. This building should be carefully placed in terms of the garden's scenery. In the Garden of Delight, the Chamber of Delight is located to the north of the site to take advantage of the garden's view to the south. Because it is built behind rocky hills, visitors cannot see the entire building from the entrance. This arrangement follows the general rule that the best views in the garden should be hidden by something. This functions in the same way as a shadow wall in a dwelling, preventing evil Qi from entering the space. The apartment itself should be two stories high and feature a deck from which a more distant view of the garden can be enjoyed.

The roof of the Chamber of Delight should be single-layered, half-gabled, and half-pitched. As is the case in the Ancestral Temple, the four corners of the roof feature "Flying Swallow" eaves. This type of high-flared roof is one of the main features that distinguish the buildings of southern China from those of northern China, and it is especially found in gardens. Compared with the roof of the temple, the decoration on the roof ridges will be much simpler, and no dragon figures can be used. On the two ends of the central ridge pole, abstract bird figures are applied, as is the case on the roof of the main hall in houses. The ridge pole itself will be decorated with abstract figures of bats ("fu") to represent happiness.

Another important type of structure within the garden is the pavilion. In Chinese, a pavilion is called a "ting," which also means "stop." As this definition implies, a pavilion is a place to rest from walking, to meditate, or to play chess with friends. Pavilions can be built at the corner of a courtyard or in the middle of an archway. In most cases, they are built beside a water pond or on top of a hill. As pavilions are built for rest, which is associated with calmness, they are dominated by the Yin force. Water, on the other hand, is associated with the Yang force. As a result of this combination of Yin and Yang forces, it is very auspicious to have waterside pavilions in gardens.

Pavilions can be built in many different shapes and sizes. In the Garden of Delight, there are rectangular, square, octagonal, and fan-shaped ones. The roof is the most important element of a pavilion. It can be half-gabled, half-pitched, four-pitched, or in other styles. The roofs feature exuberantly upturned eaves so that the pavilions themselves become part of the scenery.

Painted pavilion bridge, Beijing.

Interior view of the Imperial Garden, Beijing, showing pavilions.

ARCADES

The arcade is one of the most important structures within a garden. This winding route leads visitors to discover previously hidden scenes. The roof of an arcade is double-pitched and is

Overview of the arcade in the
Garden of Delight *(model)*.

View of a typical pavilion facade.

supported directly by pillars. The space between the two pillars can be either open or enclosed by walls. If it is open, there will be a latticework under the purlins and on the balustrades. If closed, the wall of the arcade will feature picturesque openings or grilles. In elevation the arcade presents a rhythm of solid and void, and its characteristic feature is the zigzag shape.

Not only was water in gardens not allowed to run in a straight line but historically other objects in gardens also use winding lines to retain beneficial Qi. The paths, walls, bridges, and covered walkways were all designed to undulate in plan or elevation. The covered-walkway near the entrance was divided into several sections to enhance the space's complexity. Between the Green Shadow Pavilion and the Water Pavilion, for example, a latticework screen was placed to divide the space in half and thus increase its ambiguity. The route between the Winding Brook Building and the West Building was even more varied through inclusion of the zigzag corridor, and through the changing views afforded by the openings in the walls. The spaces in the "Crane Place" were sometimes closed and sometimes open in order to intrigue visitors with the ever evolving spatial patterns. The course of the visiting route changed directions several times between its poles—the Five Mountain Immortal Building and the Raised Peak Pavilion. Like flowing Qi, the visitors "glided" through the garden spaces gracefully and gently.

Historically, gardens also utilized forms that enhanced and retained beneficial Qi. In Zhuozhengyuan, for example, a covered walkway was designed to feature as many changes of direction as possible. Similarly, the entrance to the Yuyuan garden of Shanghai was purposely designed to exclude evil Qi. Winding lines are also associated with the dragon, the most potent symbol of Chinese geomancy. It was believed that dragons resided in mountain ranges and that they had the power to cause rain to fall. To honor the dragon force, a wall was decorated with a dragon head in Yuyuan in Shanghai. Similarly, a gate was guarded by an image of a dragon in a garden in Shanyuan. The famous garden of Liuyuan also provides a good example to illustrate consideration of Qi. From the entrance, whether you turned to the west or to the east, the winding, covered walkway and irregularly placed buildings combined to enhance the perceived complexity of the spaces within the garden. As a result, Qi flew between the spaces without dispersing.

View of the arcade entrance, Yuyuan, Shanghai.

OTHER GARDEN BUILDINGS

Gardens also typically include some courtyard buildings. The courtyard buildings that are placed near to the garden's entrance are similar to dwellings. Those located in the inner

View of the Garden of Delight (model).

part of the garden, however, are different. As noted earlier, courtyards in a dwelling are symmetrically laid out to reflect the order of human society (itself thought to be a mirror of the ordered universe). The inner part of the garden, in contrast, is thought to be a retreat world for Daoists. This area's quality is mystical and abstruse. Here there is a constant exchange of Yin and Yang forces. The single enclosed courtyard form is, therefore, broken, and several courtyards are combined together. At the northeast corner of the Garden of Delight, for example, four small courtyards are interlocked. The courtyard spaces are separated by exterior partition walls, but the window grilles, and other types of openings, enable visitors to catch glimpses of what is beyond. When looking through the openings from different angles, the view is forever changing. As a result, an illusion of great depth can be created.

GARDEN BUILDING INTERIORS

Garden building interiors are designed as forms through which to view the scenes outside. Views of nature are to be taken in from the garden interiors, and from the furniture that is placed in garden courtyards. The floors of buildings are made of either stone or terra cotta. As in dwellings, the entrances of the buildings in the garden open to the south. On the southern walls many windows are included. Both the door and window openings are decorated with delicate latticework. The silhouette of this latticework serves both to separate and connect the interior and exterior.

The arrangement of garden furniture will be solemn and stately in the main garden halls, such as the Chamber of Delight. The altar table will be placed on the central axis of the hall against a solid wall. A miniature landscape representing the "Three Isles of the Blessed" can be placed on the altar table. The chairs in the seating area will be arranged in a square shape. The tables in interiors will either be round or in a long rectangular shape. Round ones are ideal for groups of people to have conversations, drink tea, play chess, or write poems. Long tables are used to display lacquer boxes, brilliant porcelain pieces, and miniature gardens. The chairs used in these spaces are of two kinds. Long-backed ones are set against a wall or are placed in the center of the room. Low-back chairs are placed against walls with windows. Miniature gardens and landscapes must be included in garden interiors. They are the means through which the the interiors communicate with the natural world outside. Plants within the spaces can be placed either directly on tables or on plant stands.

PATHS AND BRIDGES

The most important characteristics of the paths in the garden is their winding nature. As in the arcade, winding paths will stop the straight flow of malevolent Qi. The paths feature pebbles in various designs, and have similar motifs to those used in the the design of window grilles. Circles, rectangles, petals, and the abstract shapes of fish and other animals are repeated here to show the consistency of the world from macro to micro scale.

The bridges in the garden can be built either of rock or wood. Natural rock bridges are used to span narrow water courses, as a reflection of the great beauty of the natural world. Long bridges across wider water surfaces are built of wood and should change direction frequently. "Nine turn bridges" are common and are consistent with the nine turn river near Mount Kunlun. This kind of bridge often features a covered roof, like those found in the arcade. The structural system and decorative forms are the same as those found in the arcade too.

5

Emerging trends in Western design

The Village of Long Happiness provides an example of the many layers of complexity and meaning that underpin traditional Chinese architecture and design. In contrast, one of the primary criticisms of recent Western architecture has been that it lacks meaning. Since the mid-1960s a range of approaches have developed that attempt to address this problem in an effort to recapture the richness of preindustrial designing. The architecture and design of preindustrial times were inextricably linked to the cultures they served. It is not possible, or desirable even, to return to the social conditions that prevailed before the industrial era. It is not likely, either, that culture and cultural production will ever again be as unified as they were in traditional societies,

SITE. Best Products Company Forest Showroom, Richmond, Virginia, 1980. The building was constructed in a densely wooded suburban area and was sited so as not to destroy existing vegetation. The forest is allowed to actually penetrate and envelop the showroom via a thirty-five-foot gap between the facade and the actual front wall of the store. Customers make the connection to the building on foot by passing through the glass storefront of the outer facade and crossing a bridge to enter the showroom. *(Courtesy SITE Environmental Design, New York)*

SITE. Isuzu Space Station, Yokahama, Japan, **1989. Rendering.** This project was sponsored by the Isuzu Motors company and Japan Railway for the Yokohama Exotic Showcase '89, and it was intended to celebrate people's relationship to space exploration. SITE's concept treats the entire plaza surface as though it was a void in the universe — all the objects and pedestrians that might occupy a conventional street are turned upside down, so they appear to be weightless and/or in contact with an invisible surface established above the actual plaza paving. *(Courtesy SITE Environmental Design, New York)*

or as much as modernists hoped they would be afterward. Instead, we should try to determine how some of the experiential qualities that have been lost in the headlong adoption of technology might be reintroduced to our present context. There is no straightforward way to do this. Rather, we must be content, as Belgian architect Lucien Kroll says of his own attempts to foster collaboration in the architectural design process, to "progress from mistake to mistake."[1]

A range of architects, designers, and theorists have developed approaches to make design more responsive to its users and more responsible to the various contexts in which it is situated. Three of the primary concerns that have emerged are:

1. Ecological responsiveness
2. The quest for higher meaning
3. Consideration of the use and experience of design

In the section that follows, the characteristics of each of these trends, and the thoughts of the principal advocates of each, will be reviewed. In addition, the ways in which traditional Chinese thought informs and, in many cases, goes beyond current thinking in the West will also be set out. This comparison is particularly relevant as many of the new trends in Western designing — such as placing more emphasis on the processes of making and use than on the "product" as an artifact — are presaged by Daoist thought. Explicit consideration of these philosophical beliefs can broaden and deepen our thinking about how to improve the quality of design as the millennium approaches.

SITE. Isuzu Space Station, Yokahama, Japan, **1989.** Wines differentiates SITE's work from much other Green Design, noting that the term "can refer to the lingering 1960s advocacy of minimal-tech-geodesic domes, mud-brick houses, solar dwellings, and isolated communes, that rejects any association with the dreaded industrial/military insanity. There are the ecoglobal unifiers who propose that habitat should be linked, like ecology itself, to an infinitely complex, worldwide functional system designed to create a universal community of shared resources. Then there is the garden crowd where 'green' means trees and a conviction that salvation of humanity is based on less building and more planting." *(Image courtesy SITE Environmental Design, New York; text quoted in Crosbie 1994: 118)*

Ecological responsiveness

Perhaps the best known, and most discussed, of these new design trends is *Green Design*, an approach that features offshoots such as Design-for-Disassembly and Life-Cycle Design.[2] Green Design, in its various guises, and applied to all different scales of designing, is based on an acknowledgement that all design outcomes, in particular architecture, are tremendously resource intensive—both to build and to operate over time. Further, buildings, for example, don't last forever, and their materials must be disposed of upon their demolition. Along the way, as well, mistakes will be made, an example being the use of toxic materials such as asbestos; at some point these will have to be removed in as benign a way as possible, though in many cases much damage will already have been done. Though concern with the environmental impact of design is overdue, and it is such a big problem that even an incremental improvement will be of benefit, many of the current responses to the subject are quite limited. Often, for example, architects want to do "green" architecture, *not* suggest to their clients that perhaps a new building is not necessary. Another common response is to adopt an aesthetic approach introducing, for example, foliage, curved walls, and organic materials, rather than, to adapt Le Corbusier's metaphor, turning buildings into energy-efficient green "machines." The architecture firm SITE has adopted a fairly visually based Green Design approach, though they do not focus solely on formal considerations. James Wines, a founding principal of the firm,

SITE. Ross's Landing Plaza and Park, Chattanooga, Tennessee, 1992. SITE's concept for this project was that the main site area be treated as a microcosm of the entire city—including its urban grid and flowing landscape. To create a metaphorically readable and visually appealing equivalent for the township, the site is articulated by a series of thirty-five longitudinal ribbons of paving, water, and vegetation. *(Courtesy SITE Environmental Design, New York)*

SITE. Ross's Landing Plaza and Park, Chattanooga, Tennessee, 1992. Wines says further of green design that "the term 'green' can also refer to the 'deep' ecologists who believe that all industrialized living should be curbed in favor of a retreat to Aboriginal-like resourcefulness in nature. . . . In addition, there is the cutting edge of environmental technologists [whose] buildings are catalog checklists of the latest innovations in low-energy heating, cooling, and construction techniques. Obviously, all of these groups frequently share each other's territories; at the same time, however, there is a kind of competitive 'clubiness' and factionalism that persists in the green movement." *(Image courtesy SITE Environmental Design, New York; text quoted in Crosbie 1994: 118)*

SITE. Japan Cultural Center, Paris, France, 1990. Competition entry. The project was planned with the view that the Japan Cultural Center in Paris should be a symbolic microcosm of French and Japanese architecture and landscape. The structure is a narrative statement that fuses nature, buildings, and the Zen garden. *(Courtesy SITE Environmental Design, New York)*

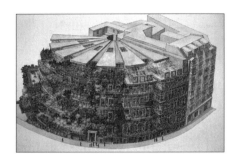

SITE. Japan Cultural Center, Paris, France, 1990. Competition entry. Further clarifying SITE's position within the Green Design spectrum, Wines says, "In this somewhat embattled area, SITE's work could probably be categorized as the 'art wing' of ecosensibility in architecture. It is our conviction that an awareness of ecology is as much a social and esthetic concept as it is an acknowedgment of nature's integrated processes. We believe, quite simply, that when environmental technology is used in a structure it should be expressed through clear visual means in the final design and that all architecture today should connect in some creative way to its larger context — meaning social, psychological, topographical, botanical, and historical influences." *(Image courtesy SITE Environmental Design, New York; text quoted in Crosbie 1994: 118)*

in an article titled "Inside outside: The aesthetic implications of green design," noted the relationship of emerging thinking on Green Design to Eastern thought and design. Addressing traditional Japanese gardens, for example, Wines noted:

> From their origins in the 15th century, these "landscapes of the mind" were infused with spiritual and intellectual values that produced a timeless power of communication. They extended the Buddhist belief in the garden as a microcosm of a larger universe and as an embodiment of inside/outside. This is also a condition found in the Japanese architecture embracing these gardens. Here, duality is expressed by the flow of space from interior to exterior and by the tissue-like membrane walls separating the two. It was this impressive Japanese achievement that profoundly influenced Frank Lloyd Wright and became the foundation for his philosophy of organic architecture.[3]

It is this organic inside/outside quality that underpins much of SITE's recent work. There are certainly arguments to be made in favor of adoption of visual metaphors, such as these, from nature into architectural design, particularly as a way of "softening" the hard edges of environments and introducing an evolving layer of richness that is not possible with fixed geometries. Green Design is so important, however, that designers should not restrict themselves to aesthetic considerations.

In product design, where the objects are smaller but their numbers are greater, two of the most widespread of the developing trends are Design-for-Disassembly and Life-Cycle Design. With these approaches, the broader implications of design decisions are considered—not just, as is traditional, the phases of marketing and use. At the outset of the design process the need for a product is considered, and, where possible, recycled and recyclable materials are used in the design. The various parts of the product are coded, indicating the materials they are made of and their suitability for recycling. In addition, products are assembled in such a way that they can be quickly and easily disassembled when the product reaches the end of its useful life. This "cradle to grave" thinking is slowly replacing the fiction that designers need consider only the immediate purpose of a product.

Within architecture, perhaps the most notable spokesperson for the green approach is William McDonough, Dean of the School of Architecture at the University of Virginia and principal

SITE. Horoscope Ring, Toyama, Japan, 1992. Model. The purpose of the project, according to SITE, was to provide a park area for the First Japan Expo in Toyama. Designed to celebrate the image of the horoscope, this sixty-two-meter-diameter circular plaza is intended to capture the mystical and symbolic connections that join the stars, the constellations, and orbits of the planets. In response to more functional considerations, there is a six-meter-wide outside ring that is designed to provide shelter and for a series of gift shops, food stores, and commercial facilities for selling souvenirs and horoscope-related artifacts. *(Courtesy SITE Environmental Design, New York)*

Horoscope Ring, Toyama, Japan, 1992. Describing SITE's own Greeen Design work, Wines says, "Virtually all of SITE's buildings and public spaces reflect the philosophy that environmentally conscious architecture should demonstrate this connection [to nature] through esthetic choices and combined visual and techical innovations. This view is supported historically by those glorious climate-conscious cities of the Middle East and India where structures sustained their beauty and relevance over the centuries by converting contextual sensitivity into high art. Our influences have been these past examples and we feel our challenge now is to continue to seek ways to bring buildings and spaces into a similar integration with the environment. For SITE, green architecture is an art, as well as a survival, imperative." *(Image courtesy SITE Environmental Design; New York; text quoted in Crosbie 1994: 118)*

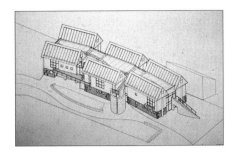

William McDonough + Partners. Frankfurt Child Care Competition, 1991. Axonometric. Modeled on ancient archetypes, such as adobe walls and Bedouin tents, this building is designed to emphasize the utilization of natural energy sources, and especially the use of daylighting for illuminating the children's activities.

William McDonough + Partners. Gap Corporate Campus, scheduled completion: late-1997. Model. This complex, for northern California, features a roof that is reminiscent of the grass-covered, rolling coastal terrain in the region in which it is situated. The focal point of the design is an original grove of oaks, one of the few remaining in the area.

William McDonough + Partners. Heinz Family Foundations Offices, 1993. Interior view. These offices, which are located in the CNG Tower in Pittsburgh, are conceived of as an open-air village. State-of-the-art environmental technologies are used, and, as this photograph illustrates, clerestory glazing is used to "soften" the effect of the design by bringing daylight to the interiors.

of the Charlottesville, Virginia, based architectural firm William McDonough + Partners. He is both a polemicist, arguing convincingly for the adoption of Green Design principles by architects and suppliers, and a practitioner, having designed a wide variety of buildings in various parts of the world. McDonough set out his view of architects' and designers' responsibility in "Design, ecology, ethics and the making of things: A centennial sermon," which was delivered at the Cathedral of St. John the Divine in New York City in 1993. He explained:

> If we understand that design leads to the manifestation of human intention, and if what we make with our hands is to be sacred and honor the earth that gives us life, then the things we make must not only rise from the ground but return to it, soil to soil, water to water, so everything that is received from the earth can be freely given back without causing harm to any living system. This is ecology. This is good design. It is of this we must now speak.[4]

McDonough has drafted a manifesto for Green Design titled "The Hannover Principles" that presents specific environmental considerations that architects should take into account in their work. They are:

1. *Insist on rights of humanity and nature to co-exist* in a healthy, supportive, diverse and sustainable condition.

2. *Recognize interdependence.* The elements of human design interact with and depend upon the natural world, with broad and diverse implications at every scale. Expand design considerations to recognizing even distant effects.

3. *Respect relationships between spirit and matter.* Consider all aspects of human settlement including community, dwelling, industry and trade in terms of existing and evolving connections between spiritual and material consciousness.

4. *Accept responsibility for the consequences of design* decisions upon human well-being, the visibility of natural systems, and their right to co-exist.

5. *Create safe objects of long-term value.* Do not burden future generations with requirements for maintenance or vigilant administration of potential danger due to the careless creation of products, processes, or standards.

6. *Eliminate the concept of waste.* Evaluate and optimize the full life-cycle of products and processes, to approach the state of natural systems, in which there is no waste.

7. *Rely on natural energy flows.* Human designs should, like the living world, derive their creative forces from perpetual solar income. Incorporate this energy efficiently and safely for responsible use.

8. *Understand the limitations of design.* No human creation lasts forever and design does not solve all problems. Those who create and plan should practice humility in the face of nature. Treat nature as a model and mentor, not an inconvenience to be evaded or controlled.

9. *Seek constant improvement by the sharing of knowledge.* Encourage direct and open communication between colleagues, patrons, manufacturers and users to link long term sustainable considerations with ethical responsibility, and re-establish the integral relationship between natural processes and human activity.

The Hannover Principles should be seen as a living document committed to the transformation and growth in the understanding of our interdependence with nature, so that they may adapt as our knowledge of the world evolves.[5]

As with any evolving trend, however, advocates can take their principles to an extreme. In the case of Green Design, this

William McDonough + Partners. Oberlin College Environmental Studies Center, scheduled completion: late 1998. Model view. This building, which is to house classrooms, an auditorium, and a library, is intended to be used as a pedagogical tool to encourage students to be mindful of materials selection, water use, and wastewater recycling.

William McDonough + Partners. Oberlin College Environmental Studies Center, scheduled completion: late 1998. Section model. This model illustrates the care taken to "embed" energy-efficient technologies in the building, making them the central feature guiding the design process.

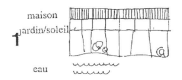

1 maison
   jardin/soleil

   eau

2 eau/jardin

   maison

3 maison
   rue
   face avant
   verger ?
   maison
   jardin

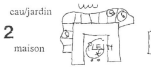
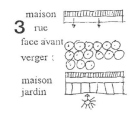

COMPOSANTS

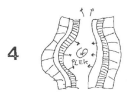

4

   lieu central   porte
   étroit

   jardin/maison/espace central/maison/jardin

5

   chaleur ou ouvert
   îlot fermé

  la tour d'observation

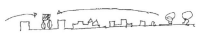

6 maisons/vert

Lucien Kroll. Ecolonia. Diagrams of patterns for ecological town planning, used in the development of Ecolonia in Alphen-aan-den-Rijn, the Netherlands. *(Courtesy Lucien Kroll)*

Lucien Kroll. Ecolonia. Alphen-aan-den-Rijn, the Netherlands. Though it is not his exclusive concern, Kroll does orient houses to the south, as here, if other landscape features and social considerations can also be accommodated. *(Courtesy Lucien Kroll)*

involves allowing consideration of the physical environment to dictate design decision making to the near exclusion of all other issues. Lucien Kroll, in describing his own firm's Green Design work, emphasizes that it is necessary to balance ecological principles with other concerns, considering all of the "ecologies" to be affected by designing. He notes:

> All of the environmental considerations should be part of what we try to do, but we have so little information about that, and it's not organized. The consumption of energy, the polluting index, for example, we don't know. We guess and it's dangerous because ancient materials seem always healthier than new ones, which is not rational, but it's a habit. That is one thing, it's a minimum. What seems much more important is that we don't have the image of boxes which have been prefabricated and laid down with the form of the industry, not the form of society. Ecology is much more than that: everything should be related to everything else and these relationships should give the form, not the process of prefabrication or the logic of having everyone face the south.
>
> Some ecological projects in Holland, for instance, propose identical houses, all with the facade to the south, which destroys the town. That is the military rank, that is not ecology for us, even if it spares energy. Having more sun is agreeable, but we want to avoid the cold organization of one logic. A "chaotic" urban tissue is more ecological than parallel houses toward the sun! So the cross-fertilization of orientation to the sun, trees, shrubs, greenery, interrelated inhabitants, climbing plants — that co-habitation between nature, not as a myth alone, but also as a reality with an impact inside your bedroom, with these things that remind you every minute that you are part of that — that's what we want.[6]

Lucien Kroll. Lycée d'Enseignement Professionnel Industriel, Belfort, France. Here Kroll nestled the school he designed into the existing landscape (the multifaceted roof is seen just above the hill) in contrast to the existing tower blocks that disregard the site's unique characteristics. *(Courtesy Lucien Kroll)*

This more wholistic quality of Green Design represents a true merging with nature, not just an evocation of its appearance. By sharing, as Daoists do, nature's operating principles — such as evolution, growth, and complexity — design becomes truly responsive. These attributes strongly recall Daoist philosophy and its manifestations in built form. As pioneers such as SITE, McDonough, and Kroll are demonstrating, designers *can* integrate their work with nature, embodying to varying degrees its processes through their actions. Their work serves as a reminder that it is not enough to attempt to "go back to nature." Instead, we must use the tools available to us now in order to achieve a reconciliation with our natural environment.

The quest for higher meaning

As noted earlier, one of the central topics of discussion in design has been the lack of meaning of much design since modernism. This problem emerged with the onset of industrialism when the modernists sought a "clean slate" through which to reform culture through architecture. It was essential, in their view, that they eschew the forms of the past — to the extent that Le Corbusier wanted not simply to change Paris but to replace it altogether with his "Radiant City." Similarly, the Futurists wanted to fill in the canals of Venice so that the inefficient waterways could be replaced by roads.[7]

The postmodernists, led by the theories of Robert Venturi, rightly rejected the antihistorical stance of the modernists, recognizing the need to reintroduce into architecture preindustrial symbols and forms that people are familiar with. The arbitrary and eclectic appliqué of postmodernism, however, often as not also leads to alienation of users, driven as it is by fashion-conscious caprice rather than by a genuine attempt to evoke people's cultural memory. Though the postmodernists correctly identified the key failing of late-twentieth-century architecture — its inherent lack of meaning — their solution of applied symbolism does not provide a sufficient response to the problem.

More recently a number of architects have explored the application of literary theories of "deconstruction" to architecture in order, through form, to reflect the alienation that they feel underlies present-day culture. Architects, such as Peter Eisenman, Zaha Hadid, and Daniel Libeskind, may, in fact, be largely correct in their analysis of the cultural condition we presently face in the West. They may also produce brilliant sculptural forms, but what purpose is served, other than polemical, in an architecture whose very intention is to symbolize a lack of meaning?

Looking beyond the "high-style" architecture that dominates the design debate but that in fact accounts for a very small fraction of the buildings in the world, what do we find? The situation in the United States is summed up with brutal accuracy by designer and theorist John Rheinfrank:

> I go through a suburb and see these garbage tract houses that are being built in these neighborhoods with essentially no human contact, even among family members, because of the layout of the house. That's criminal. We somehow have worked ourselves into a frenzy about how extraordinary these $500,000 houses are, but they're ghettos — just emotional and intellectual ghettos.[8]

Remedying this pervasive lack of meaning in contemporary architecture is not, however, an easy task. The conditions that prevailed in preindustrial times have changed, and there is no longer a shared set of cultural beliefs that can be "embedded" into design to give it meaning. Viewed in this way, the deconstructivists solution — symbolizing the "dislocation" that is characteristic of late-twentieth-century culture in the West — seems to be almost all right. But, considered more thoroughly, it seems that some attempt to find a design language (or languages) appropriate to this period would be a more useful approach.

A few design approaches have begun to explicitly consider the meanings and, in some cases, the spiritual content, of buildings, artifacts, and "intangible" products, such as computer software. Interpretive design is one such approach, developed by Michael McCoy and his students at Cranbrook Academy, during the course of his 25-year-long tenure there. With this approach, designers use visual metaphors to "signal" to potential users the purpose or function of the object they are encountering. This is particularly important in application to novel design tasks involving microchip-based equipment, such as computers and answerphones, that possess few physical constraints to guide designing. The Interpretive design approach can be extended so that visual metaphors not only inform potential users of a product's purpose but also guide them through its use.[9]

Many other people have also explored ways of infusing meaning and spiritual quality into designing, including: Christopher Day, who believes that design should be viewed as a "healing art"[10]; Victor Papanek, who argues for a reintroduction of explicit spiritual component into design[11]; and, of course, Christopher Alexander, whose buildings, books, and theories are based on an abandonment of the arid intellectual formalism of mainstream architecture and design and the embracing of the forms and feelings of preindustrial times in contemporary architecture.[12] Addressing this point in a debate with deconstructivist Peter Eisenman, Alexander said:

> I really cannot conceive of a properly formed attitude toward buildings, as an artist or builder, or in any way, if it doesn't ultimately confront the fact that buildings work in the realm of feeling.... Actually, it's been my impression that a large part of the history of modern architecture has been a kind of panicked withdrawal from these kinds of feelings, which have governed the formation of buildings over the last 2,000 years or so.[13]

This quality of feeling, which is central to the pattern language that Alexander developed with his team at the Center for Environmental Structure, was described very clearly in the classic text *The timeless way of building*. Alexander wrote:

> Those of us who are concerned with buildings tend to forget too easily that all the life and soul of a place, all of our experiences there, depend not simply on the physical environment, but on the patterns of events which we experience there.... We know, then, that what matters in a building or a town is not its outward shape, its physical geometry alone, but the events that happen there.... The action and the space are indivisible. The action is supported by this kind of space. The space supports this kind of action. The two form a unit, a pattern of events in space.... But in our time the languages have broken down. Since they are no longer shared, the processes which keep them deep have broken down: and it is therefore virtually impossible for anybody, in our time to make a building live.[14]

Alexander's notion of pattern languages has not only been used by himself, and his team, in their building projects but also by others who have applied the idea to a variety of tasks, such as furniture and computer software design. All of these applications of the pattern language concept are done in order to create "wholeness," or living environments — that "just right" relationship of people to the contexts in which they interact.

There is no doubt that much recent architecture and design is alienating and that the processes that mainstream designers use do not lead to wholeness. The various attempts to make architecture and design more meaningful, and to give them more spiritual content, are to be applauded. In the proliferation of such approaches, as well, there is a hidden wisdom — it will not be possible to have the type of unified design approach in the future that characterized preindustrial times. It is *very* unlikely that there will ever again be a core set of shared beliefs within any culture. Designers must now, instead, attempt to respond to the many rapidly changing subcultures of interest that exist within society. These will at some times be complementary, and at other times they will be in conflict. As British musician and artist Brian Eno noted in a survey of cultural trends, it is time to "start thinking of identity as something multiple, shifting, blurred, experimental and adaptive."[15]

Eno's assessment is probably quite accurate, but the question remains, how can an architect or designer possibly create meaning in such a fluid situation? Daoist philosophy can help Western designers tremendously here. There *is* a hunger for meaning and for a spiritual basis for design. This desire is, however, inarticulate — it springs from a broader dissatisfaction that arises from the absence of these qualities in the culture as a whole. In other words, people have a general sense of what is lacking but no firm idea of how to fill the void. Designers can help here, not by anticipating or reflecting back evanescent cultural trends but by adopting for themselves a core set of beliefs to guide their design thinking and form production. There is a fervent wish for design to reflect *something* beyond itself. Adopting, however arbitrarily, Daoist philosophical considerations (though not specifically Chinese cultural forms) as a basis for design would lead to richer designs. By working on the basis of a wholistic philosophical system such as Daoism, architects and designers would infuse their work with more meaning and spiritual content than if the designs were conceived of, as is presently the case, simply in terms of relationships of abstract geometries.

Consideration of the use and experience of design

In addition to environmental responsiveness and the quest for higher meaning, there is also an increasing emphasis on the quality of experience that interaction with design gives rise to. The unsatisfactory nature of the reduction of design to manipulation of prismatic geometry, that began in the modern era and that has persisted since, has become readily apparent. In the face of this, a number of designers and theorists are paying more explicit attention in their work to the quality of design experience and to the efficacy of design in use.

One of the first to address this topic was Danish architect and writer Steen Eiler Rasmussen, who wrote the classic book *Experiencing architecture* that first appeared in English in 1959. Rasmussen departs from the geometrical focus of much mainstream architectural history and considers the different aspects of users' experience of buildings. One chapter, for example, is titled "Hearing Architecture."[16] Architects and designers need to redevelop this type of awareness — one that takes into account the totality of users' experience — if design is to be truly whole and satisfying.

The actual quality of spaces — what goes on there, and how it feels — has also been receiving more attention in recent years than in the past. One particularly interesting approach to this topic has been the adaptation of methods from phenomenological philosophy to an analysis of different types of spaces, and to a range of users' experiences of them. David Seamon has been a leader in this effort and has presided over the development of a collection of phenomenological literature with an environmental focus.[17] Ultimately, however, this approach is limited to providing subjective descriptions of environmental situations; it does *not* provide particularly helpful suggestions for how to act on these.

Within design practice itself, however, some have begun to make an explicit consideration of users' environmental experience the very basis of their firms' work. Italian designer and color consultant Clino Trini Castelli, for example, coined the term "The Qualistic" to describe this nonobjective, but very real, component of the environmental milieu. He explained:

Qualistic is now in the mainstream Italian vocabulary and is considered an analogy. It implies the perception of quality from a subjective point of view. Quality is by definition — from a philosophical point of view and from a certain point in our history practically starting from Galileo — a quantitative dimension, that is, one associated with quantity. It is a dimension where the perception of quality can be shared in an objective way by any person. So if I talk about color, I talk about the quality of the paint. I say, this paint can resist 10,000 hours of the sun's rays or of ultraviolet light — that is a quantitative quality. But if I talk about a certain type of color you like, you can recognize that this paint has a certain kind of quality. Another person does not recognize any quality in that color, so the qualistic is concerned with the perception of quality connected with the subjective evaluation — it is the perception of quality that changes from person to person. This dimension we have called *qualistic* in order to distinguish it from the quality that has a meaning of quantity and objectivity.[18]

Though this kind of subjective quality is also the focus of much design in the East, there is a pronounced tendency in Western culture to devalue, diminish, or simply ignore that which is nonquantifiable or intuitive. It is, however, these very qualities that have the most profound effect on how comfortable we feel in a space. In their design of exhibition spaces and software interfaces, the New York based firm Edwin Schlossberg, Inc., also focuses on the quality of user experience. Schlossberg uses the metaphor "creating conversations" to describe his firm's work. Addressing the process they use to achieve this, he said:

So the position or the place that I always start from in working on projects is: What can I do to create tools through which people can understand the world better? And what are some of the messages, ideas, and concerns that can be articulated through the experience to engage people and help them see how astonishing the world is, how interesting they are, how interesting what's going on in their head is, as they experience these things?… [T]he most interesting things we do are as a result of a conversation with other people. Sometimes the conversation is sort of a delayed-feedback conversation, where a scientist discovers an idea and we create a context through which that idea can be communicated so others understand it. Or it can be

Bernard Tschumi. "Part Four: The Block." From *The Manhattan Transcripts*. Diagrams of different types of movement in space. *(Courtesy of Bernard Tschumi)*

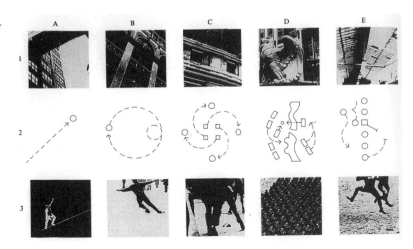

something where the tool that's in the physical space serves as an experience on the basis of which you can understand the person standing next to you better. The most powerful experiences are ones in which you sort of elbow the person next to you and say, "Did you see that?" or "Can you believe that?" or "I never understood anything like that." So, always my hope is to create tools that enable people to have that kind of interaction and conversation with other people in the space.[19]

Within architecture, as well, there is a subgroup of practitioners who base their work on a consideration of the interaction between visitors and architecture. "Narrative Architecture" has been practiced in various forms and at different times by, among others, Bernard Tschumi, Nigel Coates, Hans Hollein, and the firm SITE.[20] The focus of this approach is to create a "score" of the events that are to take place in a space over time. At other times these architects diagram the experiences that visitors to the space are to have and provide a formal "foil" to support these activities. Swiss-French architect and educator Bernard Tschumi was one of the first to diagrammatically highlight the effect of movement in space in his 1978 project *The Manhattan Transcripts;* he has used this movement as the conceptual basis for much of his subsequent work. Another, perhaps more readily comprehensible, example of this approach can be found in Hans Hollein's design for an Austrian Travel Bureau office in Vienna. In this case, Hollein arranged a flowing spatial sequence within which each activity (for example, rail travel or air travel) was given its own area, in the likely order that visitors might want to use them. Each space was also assigned formal cues to indicate its purpose. There were, for example, sculptural birds above the air travel counter and, at the last stop on the sequence, Rolls-Royce grilles in front of the cashiers' windows. In this way visitors's experience, the choreography of their visit, and the formal elements needed to support those activities were all explicitly considered in the design process.

Recently quite a number of people have started to explore this territory in their work, introducing metaphors and processes by which the experiential quality of space and its evolving use over time are made the very basis of design. British architect and author Frank Duffy, for example, makes the comparison between "hardware" and "software" thinking in design.[21] Conventional design thinking, since the advent of modernism, has focused almost entirely on the "hardware" side — the building as an object or a physical artifact. Instead of this, Duffy argues, we need to adopt a "software" focus, considering the ways in which uses of design change over time. In this way we can build in, from the very beginning of the design process, the flexibility to cope with these changes. Duffy discussed the relationship between the hardware and software views of designing in terms of the work of his firm, DEGW International. He said:

> It's an interesting analogy and a very important one, I think, for architects. . . . It's essential to get architects to understand the importance of the designing of the use of space through time. This concept allows architects to deal with the questions of obsolescence, it allows us to deal with the way in which buildings mature, it allows us to deal with managerial issues, it gives us much, much greater scope than we would have otherwise as designers.[22]

A further evolution of this software concept has been developed by Stewart Brand who has adapted the use of "scenario planning" to the design process. The scenario approach was originally developed by Peter Schwartz, President of the Global Business Network, for use as a business forecasting tool.[24] Scenarios are used not to predict the future but to imagine, based on what is known today, the way in which circumstances might change in the future. Brand uses scenario planning to enable architects to see that it is not their job to plan inviolable artifacts but instead to acknowledge that circumstances, needs, and the uses of buildings are always changing. If these cannot be anticipated, at least designs should allow for this evolution to take place as smoothly as possible. Christopher Alexander's concept of "repair" is also consistent with this idea.[25] He insists that architects should use construction techniques that allow for adaptation to unforeseen changes in circumstances, something that was not possible with many of the buildings of the 1960s and 1970s. These were built solidly in concrete to suit specific functions or perceived needs that, themselves, proved not be be static. In many cases total demolition was the only remedy available.[26]

So, from this analysis, the reason for the unsatisfactory nature of so much recent Western design becomes clear. A great deal of effort and intelligence are applied by designers in their work, but, unfortunately, much of that effort is wasted because the majority of design activity is based on an incorrect understanding of the fundamental nature of the design task. Mainstream architectural methods, which rely heavily on the use of two-dimensional drawings, lead architects to pretend that buildings are static, geometrical artifacts (that is, sculptures), when in fact they are living and evolving. Similarly, people and their ways of interacting with space are not static. Unfortunately, the nature of these complex interrelationships are scarcely considered in the mainstream design process at all. To borrow a term from the deconstructivists, it is this "disjunction" between the picture of the world that most designers act upon and the nature of the situation as it actually evolves over time that causes the alienation that so many people feel from the environments and artifacts of postindustrial culture.

What is needed in architecture and design today is a fundamental reappraisal—one in which the integration of designing, not just with the physical environment but with all of the contexts in which it is situated, is explicitly considered from the outset. Further, the impact of design activity must also be addressed—do the approaches or philosophies or methods being used lead to wholeness? Are users' activities and experiences not just thought about but made the focus of the design process? A number of innovative practitioners have made progress with their work in each of these areas, but for the quality of design as a whole to improve, all of these considerations must be made central to Western design thinking.

Here again the wholistic focus of Daoist philosophy, and its manifestation in built form, provides an example that Western designers can look to for inspiration. As noted earlier, it is not appropriate to copy the forms of another time and culture, and it is not possible to return to the past. Instead, we must use the tools and technology of the present as the very means to reintroduce responsiveness and meaning. By adopting, however arbitrarily, Daoist thought as a basis for design, or at least as a framework for considering the broader implications of design at the outset of designing, we can begin to reintroduce to the piecemeal and fragmented culture of the West some of the wholistic qualities of the past.

Those who argue that architecture and design are potentially critically important cultural activities are absolutely right. In this century in the West, however, by trivializing their content, the design professions have abdicated this role. Daoist design, on the other hand, provides an example of the type of all encompassing, but supporting, role that these forms of cultural production can have in a society. There are many things that can be learned from "indwelling" with Daoist thought, but perhaps the first thing Western architects and designers should adopt is a quieter, more modest, and more contextual approach to designing. It well may be that traditional architecture speaks so clearly to us now because it does not raise its voice.

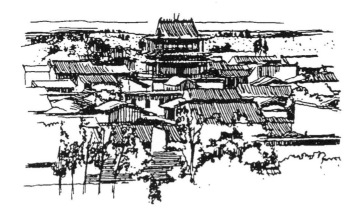

6

Conclusion

Implicit in traditional Chinese architecture and design is a wisdom presently lacking in the West. Instead of addressing the parts of the design milieu individually, every action is informed by a living philosophy that, at every stage, is devoted to creating wholeness and harmony. There is an integration of nature into all design decisions, as well as a strong cultural understanding of its importance. The emphasis is on the totality of the design experience, and not just on form alone; explicit attention is paid to the flow of energy, or Qi, within spaces of all scales to address the psychological experience of those who interact with space. The aim is to make a place, and not just a "space plan." The elements of traditional Chinese design are richly decorated, but all of the symbolism chosen has deeply rooted cultural meanings that will be understood by the vast majority of those who encounter them. Related to this use of symbolism is the spiritual quality that is infused into even the most pragmatic spaces. The pattern and process of everyday life are seemlessly supported by the outcomes of design activity. Designing and living are made harmonious by adherence to, and understanding of, the tenets of Daoist philosophy.

There is much that Western architects and designers can learn from examining the processes that give rise to traditional Chinese architecture and design, and the philosophies that underpin it. The most fundamental conclusion may be that the processes used by designers in the West may themselves be to blame for the shortcomings that have been identified in this book. It may well be that, if any significant improvement in the quality of Western design is to be achieved, a more wholistic and integrated approach, like that found in the East, will be needed. John Chris Jones addressed this point in another context. He asked:

> At what point do we recognise that centralized designing ceases to be effective and becomes an obstacle, and not the means, to "good design." Surely there is such a point. I believe we have already passed beyond it and that it is time to rethink designing, design education, and the need for design professions, in relation to the growing dissatisfaction with technology, design, planning, and their effects. The new competence which the situation now requires is, I believe, not that of deciding the shape of a product or system but the shape of a new context or process in which everyone, not just designers or experts, is enabled to see what is needed of him or her if the form of industrial life is to get better, for everyone, and not worse. To arrive at this is not to continue to design but to do something at a different scale from that, the scale of the whole problem, the scale of decentral action, thought, and imagination.[1]

If we choose to make this transition from dealing piecemeal with the issues that face us in the West to addressing, as Jones suggests we should, the whole situation, then Daoist thought, and the architecture and design that result from its application, provide an outstanding model to follow. As Jones implies, too, Western culture has one key tool that was not readily available in preindustrial times—innovation.

Christopher Alexander's work with the pattern language demonstrates that, though it may be painstakingly slow and difficult to realize, it is possible to achieve wholeness in design in our time. Designers can continue to act expediently—blaming budgets, clients, or the zeitgeist for the poor quality and maladaptiveness of their work—or they can take responsibility for infusing their work with more meaning and richness. It is a choice that faces us now—do we create a new wholeness, or do we accept continued fragmentation? Put another way, do we wish to continue to produce the type of still born work that has characterized designing of all types for the majority of the twentieth century, or do we wish to create a new and truly responsive living architecture and design?

Endnotes

Preface

1. Lao Tzu [Laozi], 1989, *Tao Teh Ching* [Dao De Jing], translated by John C. H. Wu (Boston: Shambhala: 145).

Chapter 1. Introduction

1. For a more detailed discussion, see C. Thomas Mitchell, 1993, *Redefining designing: From form to experience* (New York: Van Nostrand Reinhold: 5–33).

2. Nikolaus Pevsner, 1963, *An outline of European architecture,* 7th edition (Harmondsworth, England: Penguin Books: 15).

3. There are a number of ironies here, not the least of which is that the avowed purpose of the modernists was to produce functional sheds devoid of aesthetic intent; of course this never really happened. The initial reaction to modernism, postmodernism, has the "shed" as its basis as well. Robert Venturi, who was the pioneer of the approach, contended that buildings should be "decorated sheds" —half modern (represented by the shed) and half postmodern (distinguished by the addition of decoration). A more extensive discussion of this notion can be found in Mitchell's *Redefining designing,* 14–21.

4. Jan Swafford, 1992, *The Vintage guide to classical music* (New York: Vintage Books: 4).

5. See, for example, the critiques in Philippe Boudon, 1972, *Lived-in architecture: Le Corbusier's Pessac revised,* translated by Gerald Onn (Cambridge, MA: MIT Press); Peter Blake, 1977, *Form follows fiasco: Why modern architecture hasn't worked* (Boston: Little, Brown); Andrea Branzi, 1988, *Learning from Milan: Design and the second modernity* (Cambridge, MA: MIT Press); and Tom Wolfe, 1981, *From Bauhaus to our house* (New York: Farrar, Straus, and Giroux).

6. From "Peter Eisenman: An Architectural Design interview by Charles Jencks," 1988, *Architectural Design* 58 (3–4): 52.

7. Alan Watts, 1995, *Become what you are*, edited by Mark Watts (Boston: Shambhala: 123).

8. For a discussion of this, see C. Thomas Mitchell, 1996, *New thinking in design: Conversations on theory and practice* (New York: Van Nostrand Reinhold).

9. Alan Watts, 1957, *The way of Zen* (New York: Pantheon: 5).

10. Alan Watts, 1995, *The Tao of philosophy: The edited transcripts* (Boston: C. E. Tuttle: 4–5).

11. For a fuller discussion of this process, see Stewart Brand, 1994, *How buildings learn: What happens after they're built* (New York: Viking).

12. Alan Watts, 1995, *The Tao of philosophy: The edited transcripts* (Boston: C.E. Tuttle: 96).

13. See, for example, the discussion of the work of architects such as Zaha Hadid and Steven Holl, most of which is unbuilt (or in the case of Hadid often unbuildable). A presentation of Hadid's work is found in *Zaha M. Hadid*, 1995, edited and photographed by Yukio Futagawa; interview by Yoshio Futagawa (Tokyo: A.D.A. Edita). Steven Holl's work and theories are set out in his book *Anchoring: Selected projects, 1975–1991*, 3rd edition, 1991 (New York: Princeton Architectural Press), and Steven Holl, *Intertwining: Selected projects, 1989–1995*, 1996 (New York: Princeton Architectural Press).

14. William McDonough is perhaps the foremost advocate of this approach. See the discussion of his work in Michael Wagner's article "Creative catalyst" in *Interiors* 152 (3), March 1993: 53–67. For a further look at the subject, see, for example, Dorothy Mackenzie, 1991, *Design for the environment* (New York: Rizzoli), and Victor J. Papanek, 1995, *The green imperative: Natural design for the real world* (New York: Thames and Hudson).

15. The discussion of the spiritual is central to Christopher Alexander's work; see, for example, his *The timeless way of building*, 1979 (New York: Oxford University Press). See also Christopher Day, 1995, *Places of the soul: Architecture and environmental design as a healing art* (London: Thorsons), and Papenek's *The green imperative*.

16. The key postmodernist texts are Robert Venturi, 1966, *Complexity and contradiction in architecture* (New York: Museum of Modern Art), and Robert Venturi, Denise Scott Brown, and Steven Izenour, 1972, *Learning from Las Vegas* (Cambridge, MA: MIT Press). Other architects who have adopted this approach include Michael Graves, Robert A. M. Stern, and the late Charles Moore.

17. Interpretive design, originally termed "product semantics," was developed by Michael McCoy and his students in the Design Department at the Cranbrook Academy of Art. This work has been widely publicized — for example in the book *Cranbrook design: The new discourse*, 1990, edited by Hugh Aldersey-Williams (New York: Rizzoli). Perhaps the key philosophical statement of the movement is Lisa Krohn and Michael McCoy's "Beyond beige: Interpretive design for the post-industrial age," 1989, *Design Issues* 5 (2) (Spring): 112–123. A discussion with McCoy is featured in Mitchell's *New thinking in design*: 2–11.

18. Among those occasionally and loosely characterized as "narrative architects" are Nigel Coates, Bernard Tschumi, Hans Hollein, and the firm SITE. For a discussion of the principles behind this approach, see, for example, Coates's essay "Street signs" in *Design after modernism: Beyond the object*, 1988, edited by John Thackara (New York: Thames and Hudson: 95–114), and Rick Poynor, 1990, *Nigel Coates: The city in motion* (New York: Rizzoli).

19. Francis Duffy and his firm DEGW International have made a study of the use of office spaces, and how they change over time, the focus of their work. See, for example, Duffy, 1992, *The changing workplace*, edited by Patrick Hannay (London: Phaidon Press), and the discussion with Duffy in Mitchell's *New thinking in design*: 26–39.

20. This issue is most clearly raised, and most thoroughly explored, in Stewart Brand, 1994, *How buildings learn: What happens after they're built* (New York: Viking).

21. An interesting recent offshoot of environment-behavior studies, which traditionally has focused on quantitative research, has been work that applies a phenomenological perspective to the study of environmental experience. The leading advocate of this approach has been David Seamon. The state of current thinking is presented in the anthologies *Dwelling, place, and environment: Toward a phenomenology of person and world*, 1985, edited by David Seamon and Robert Mugerauer (New York: Columbia University Press), and *Dwelling, seeing, and designing: Toward a phenomenological ecology*, 1993, edited by David Seamon (Albany, NY: State University of New York Press). The classic text of phenomenology and the environment is Gaston Bachelard, 1994, *The poetics of space*, translated by Maria Jolas (Boston: Beacon Press)

Chapter 2. Daoist principles

1. Fritjof Capra, 1975, *The Tao of physics: An exploration of the parallels between modern physics and Eastern mysticism* (Berkeley: Shambhala: 102).

2. For a fuller discussion of the productive and destructive process of the Five Elements, see Stephen Skinner, 1982, *The living earth manual of Feng-Shui: Chinese geomancy* (London: Routledge and Kegan Paul: 52–57.

3. See Stephen Skinner, 1982, *The living earth manual of Feng-Shui: Chinese geomancy* (London: Routledge and Kegan Paul: 52–57).

4. See *The authentic I Ching* [Yi Jing], 1987, translated by Henry Wei (North Hollywood, CA: Newcastle Publishing: 37).

5. See Lao-tsu, 1989, *The Tao Te Ching* [Dao De Jing], translated by Ellen M. Chen (New York: Paragon House: 23–27).

6. Frena Bloomfield, 1989, *The book of Chinese beliefs: A journey into the Chinese inner world* (New York: Ballantine Books: 27).

7. For a discussion of this, see Mitchell's *Redefining designing*: 7–8.

8. For a discussion of this aspect of Mies's philosophy and work, see Charles Jencks. 1985, *Modern movements in architecture*, 2nd edition (New York: Viking: 95–108).

9. *The encyclopedia of Eastern philosophy and religion: Buddhism, Hinduism, Taoism, Zen*, 1994 (Boston: Shambhala).

10. Chu Hsi, "Collected works" in *Science and civilization in China, Vol. II*, 1956, translated by Joseph Needham (Cambridge: Cambridge University Press: 477–478).

11. See Stephen Skinner, 1982, *The living earth manual of Feng-Shui: Chinese geomancy* (London: Routledge and Kegan Paul: 14–22).

12. Kahn quoted in John Peter, 1994, *The oral history of modern architecture: Interviews with the greatest architects of the twentieth century* (New York: Abrams: 215).

13. From Wing-Tsit Chan, "Man and nature in the Chinese garden" in *Chinese houses and gardens*, 1950, by Henry Inn, edited by Shao Chang Lee (New York: Bonanza Books: 36).

14. From John Chris Jones, "Opus one, number two" in *designing designing*, 1991 (London: Architecture Design and Technology Press: 153–154). Poem by P'ei Ti [Pei Di], from "The Pavilion of the Lake" in *Anthology of Chinese literature: From early times to the fourteenth century*, 1965, edited by Cyril Birch (New York: Grove Press: 222).

15. Lao Tzu [Laozi], *Tao Teh Ching* [Dao De Jing], 1989, translated by John C. H. Wu (Boston: Shambhala: 23).

16. From John Chris Jones, "Opus one, number two" in *designing designing*, 1991 (London: Architecture Design and Technology Press: 162).

Chapter 3. Feng Shui

1. See, for example, the listing of titles in the bibliography under this subject.

2. Ernest J. Eitel, 1993, *Feng Shui,* with commentary by John Michell (Singapore: Graham Brash: 4).

3. John Michell in Ernest J. Eitel, 1993, *Feng Shui,* with commentary by John Michell (Singapore: Graham Brash: Foreword).

4. Sarah Rossbach, 1983, *Feng Shui: The chinese art of placement* (New York: Dutton: 2).

5. See, for example, the discussion of this point in Stephen Skinner, 1982, *The living earth manual of Feng-Shui: Chinese geomancy* (London: Routledge and Kegan Paul: 8–13).

6. Evelyn Lip, 1990, *Feng Shui for business* (Union City, CA: Heian International: 42).

7. See, for example, the discussion of these points in Frena Bloomfield, 1989, *The book of Chinese beliefs: A journey into the Chinese inner world* (New York: Ballantine Books: 8).

8. Bruce Chatwin cites reports of a cost of $600 million US in his essay "The Chinese geomancer" in *What am I doing here?* 1989 (New York: Viking: 50).

9. Bruce Chatwin, 1989, "The Chinese geomancer" in *What am I doing here?* (New York: Viking: 51).

10. Bruce Chatwin, 1989, "The Chinese geomancer" in *What am I doing here?* (New York: Viking: 50).

11. Bruce Chatwin, 1989, "The Chinese geomancer" in *What am I doing here?* (New York: Viking: 53).

12. Bruce Chatwin, 1989, "The Chinese geomancer" in *What am I doing here?* (New York: Viking: 51).

13. Bruce Chatwin, 1989, "The Chinese geomancer" in *What am I doing here?* (New York: Viking: 54).

14. Philip Langdon, 1995, "Asia bound," *Progressive Architecture* 76 (3) (March): 86.

15. Paul Glanzrock, 1995, "Banking on Heritage at China Trust," *Facilities Design and Management* 14 (2) (February): 44–45.

16. A presentation of this belief, in its original Tibetan Buddhist context, is contained in Geshe Kelsang Gyatso's book *The joyful path of good fortune: The complete guide to the Buddhist path to enlightenment,* 2nd revised edition, 1995 (London: Tharpa Publications: 110).

17. A more detailed summary of these research findings can be found in Eric Sundstrom, 1986, *Work places: The psychology of the physical environment in offices and factories* (Cambridge; New York: Cambridge University Press: 44–47).

18. Personal communication between Andrew King and C. Thomas Mitchell, 28 May 1996.

19. Bruce Chatwin, 1989, "The Chinese geomancer" in *What am I doing here?* (New York: Viking: 51–52).

Chapter 4. Dao in design

1. From Wing-Tsit Chan, "Man and nature in the Chinese garden" in *Chinese houses and gardens,* 1950, by Henry Inn, edited by Shao Chang Lee (New York: Bonanza Books: 31).

2. From Wing-Tsit Chan, "Man and nature in the Chinese garden" in *Chinese houses and gardens,* 1950, by Henry Inn, edited by Shao Chang Lee (New York: Bonanza Books: 34–35).

3. The *Kaogongji* is a chapter that was added to the book *Zhou-li* during the Han dynasty. No English translation exists, but there is an illustrated edition in Chinese: Chen Tai, 1968, *Kao kung chi tu* (Taibei: Commericial Press).

4. Quoted in Rolf A. Stein, 1987, *The world in miniature: Container gardens and dwellings in Far Eastern religious thought,* translated by Phyllis Brooks (Stanford: Stanford University Press: 226).

5. Ann Paludan, 1991, *The Chinese Spirit Road: The classical tradition of stone tomb statuary* (New Haven: Yale University Press: 8).

6. Li Jie, 1968, *Yingzao fashi* (Taibei: Commercial Press).

7. This translation is by Jiangmei Wu. An older English language translation can be found in Herbert Allen Giles, editor, 1922, *Gems of Chinese literature* (Shanghai: Kelly and Walsh: 148).

8. Quoted in Maggie Keswick, 1978, *The Chinese garden history: History, art & architecture* (New York: Rizzoli: 196).

Chapter 5. Emerging trends in Western design

1. Lucien Kroll, "Contemporaneous architecture" in C. Thomas Mitchell, 1996, *New thinking in design: Conversations on theory and practice* (New York: Van Nostrand Reinhold: 59).

2. There has been a spate of recent books on Green Design, including, in no particular order Dorothy Mackenzie, 1991, *Design for the environment* (New York: Rizzoli); Brenda Vale and Robert Vale, 1991, *Green architecture: Design for an energy-conscious future* (Boston: Little, Brown); U.S. Congress, Office of Technology Assessment, 1992, *Green products by design: Choices for a cleaner environment* (Washington, DC: GPO); John Farmer, 1996, *Green shift: Towards a green sensibility in architecture* (Oxford: Butterworth-Heinemann); Cliff Moughtin, 1996, *Urban design: Green dimensions* (Oxford: Butterworth-Heinemann); Dianna Lopez Barnett and William D. Browning, 1995, *A primer on sustainable building* (Snowmass, CO: Rocky Mountain Institute); and Michael J. Crosbie, 1994, *Green architecture: A guide to sustainable design* (Rockport, MA: Rockport Publishers).

3. James Wines, 1991, "Inside outside: The aesthetic implications of green design," *Interior Design* 62 (11) (August): 116.

4. William McDonough, 1993, "Design, ecology, ethics and the making of things: A centennial sermon," February 7 (unpublished typescript).

5. William McDonough, 1993, "The Hannover Principles" reprinted in *Interiors* 152 (3) (March): 52.

6. Lucien Kroll, "Contemporaneous architecture" in C. Thomas Mitchell, 1996, *New thinking in design: Conversations on theory and practice* (New York: Van Nostrand Reinhold: 52).

7. See Robert Hughes's chapter "Trouble in Utopia" in *Shock of the new,* revised edition, 1991 (New York: Knopf: 164–211).

8. John Rheinfrank, 1991, from an unpublished interview with C. Thomas Mitchell.

9. See Michael McCoy, "Interpretive design" in C. Thomas Mitchell, 1996, *New thinking in design: Conversations on theory and practice* (New York: Van Nostrand Reinhold: 1–11); Lisa Krohn and Michael McCoy, 1989, "Beyond beige: Interpretive design for the post-industrial age," *Design Issues* 5 (2) (Spring): 112–123; and Hugh Aldersey-Williams, editor, 1990, *Cranbrook design: The new discourse* (New York: Rizzoli).

10. Christopher Day, 1995, *Places of the soul: Architecture and environmental design as a healing art* (London: Thorsons).

11. Victor J. Papanek, 1995, *The green imperative: Natural design for the real world* (New York: Thames and Hudson).

12. See, for example, Christopher Alexander, et al., 1977, *A pattern language: Towns, buildings, construction* (New York: Oxford University Press), and Christopher Alexander, 1979, *The timeless way of building* (New York: Oxford University Press).

13. "Contrasting concepts of harmony in architecture: Debate between Christopher Alexander and Peter Eisenman," *Lotus International* 40 (1983): 61.

14. Christopher Alexander, 1979, *The timeless way of building* (New York: Oxford University Press: 62, 65, 70, 225).

15. Brian Eno, 1996, *A year with swollen appendices* (London; Boston: Faber and Faber: 403).

16. Steen Eiler Rassmussen, 1962, *Experiencing architecture,* 2nd edition, translated by Eve Wendt (Cambridge, MA: MIT Press).

17. The pioneer of this application of phenomenology to the built environment was Gaston Bachelard, whose classic book on the subject was *The poetics of space,* translated by Maria Jolas, 1994 (Boston: Beacon Press). Two anthologies of writing that David Seamon has been involved in are David Seamon, editor, 1993, *Dwelling, seeing, and designing: Toward a phenomenological ecology* (Albany, NY: State University of New York Press), and David Seamon and Robert Mugerauer, editors, 1985, *Dwelling, place, and environment: Towards a phenomenology of person and world* (New York: Columbia University Press).

18. Clino Trini Castelli, "Design primario" in C. Thomas Mitchell, 1996, *New thinking in design: Conversations on theory and practice* (New York: Van Nostrand Reinhold: 65).

19. Edwin Schlossberg, "Creating conversations" in C. Thomas Mitchell, 1996, *New thinking in design: Conversations on theory and practice* (New York: Van Nostrand Reinhold: 72–73).

20. The origin of "scoring" people's movement through space may in fact have been Lawrence Halprin, 1969, *The RSVP cycles: Creative processes in the human environment* (New York: Braziller). The narrative architects use a similar concept but arrive at much different results. An overview of all of these architects' work can be conveniently found in Charles Jencks, 1993, *Architecture today,* 2nd edition (London: Academy Editions). Tschumi's work is well presented in three books he has authored: *Architecture and disjunction,* 1994 (Cambridge, MA: MIT Press); *Event-cities: Praxis,* 1994 (Cambridge, MA: MIT Press), and *The Manhattan transcripts,* 2nd edition, 1994 (London: Academy Editions). Coates's work is presented in Rick Poynor's book *Nigel Coates: The city in motion,* 1990 (New York: Rizzoli). Coates's views on narrative architecture can be found in his essay in titled "Street signs" in John Thackara, editor, 1988, *Design after modernism: Beyond the object* (New York: Thames and Hudson: 95–114). Hans Hollein's work is presented in *Hans Hollein, design: Man transforms,* 1989 (Vienna: Locker), and in Gianni Pettena, 1988, *Hans Hollein: Works, 1960–1988* (Milano; New York: Idea Books). SITE's work is cataloged in *SITE,* 1989 (New York: Rizzoli). An overview of their philosophy can be found in James Wines, 1987, *De-architecture* (New York: Rizzoli).

21. See Duffy's discussion of this topic in Francis Duffy, 1992, *The changing workplace,* edited by Patrick Hannay (London: Phaidon Press), and in Francis Duffy, "The choreography of change" in C. Thomas Mitchell, 1996, *New thinking in design: Conversations on theory and practice* (New York: Van Nostrand Reinhold: 26–39).

22. Francis Duffy, "The choreography of change" in C. Thomas Mitchell, 1996, *New thinking in design: Conversations on theory and practice* (New York: Van Nostrand Reinhold: 32 - 33).

23. For a discussion of scenario planning in architecture see Stewart Brand's chapter on "The scenario-buffered building" in *How buildings learn: What happens after they're built,* 1994 (New York: Viking: 178–189).

24. For a presentation of scenario planning in its original, business context, see Peter Schwartz, 1991, *The art of the long view: Planning for the future in an uncertain world* (New York: Doubleday Currency), and Peter Schwartz, "Scenario planning" in C. Thomas Mitchell, 1996, *New thinking in design: Conversations on theory and practice* (New York: Van Nostrand Reinhold: 139–148).

25. See, for example, Christopher Alexander's chapter "The process of repair" in *The timeless way of building,* 1979 (New York: Oxford University Press: 475–492).

26. For a discussion of this see C. Thomas Mitchell, 1996, *New thinking in design: Conversations on theory and practice* (New York: Van Nostrand Reinhold: xi–xxiii).

Chapter 6. Conclusion

1. John Chris Jones, 1991, *designing designing* (London: Architecture Design and Technology Press: 79).

Bibliography

Preface

Bolen, Jean Shinoda. 1979. *The Tao of psychology: Synchronicity and the self.* San Francisco: Harper and Row.

Bradbury, Ray. 1989. *Zen in the art of writing.* Santa Barbara, CA: Joshua Odell Editions.

Brinker, Helmut. 1987. *Zen in the art of painting.* Translated by George Campbell. London; New York: Arkana.

Capra, Fritjof. 1975. *The Tao of physics: An exploration of the parallels between modern physics and Eastern mysticism.* Berkeley: Shambhala.

Dreher, Diane. 1991. *The Tao of inner peace: A guide to inner and outer peace.* New York: HarperPerennial.

Edelman, Joel, and Mary Beth Crain. 1993. *The Tao of negotiation: How you can prevent, resolve, and transcend conflict in work and everyday life.* New York: HarperBusiness.

Gotz, Ignacio L. 1988. *Zen and the art of teaching.* Jericho, NY: J.L. Wilkerson Pub.

Herman, Stanley M. 1994. *The Tao at work: On leading and following.* San Francisco, CA: Jossey-Bass.

Herrigel, Eugen. 1989. *Zen in the art of archery.* Translated by R. F. C. Hull. New York: Vintage Books.

Hoff, Benjamin. 1982. *The Tao of Pooh.* New York: E.P. Dutton.

Kehoe, Brendan P. 1994. *Zen and the art of the Internet: A beginner's guide.* Englewood Cliffs, NJ: Prentice-Hall.

Lao Tzu [Laozi]. 1989. *Tao Teh Ching*. [Dao De Jing]. Translated by John C. H. Wu. Boston: Shambhala.

McPhail, Mark Lawrence. 1996. *Zen in the art of rhetoric: An inquiry into coherence*. Albany: State University of New York Press.

Mitchell, C. Thomas. 1993. *Redefining designing: From form to experience*. New York: Van Nostrand Reinhold.

Nagel, Greta K. 1994. *The Tao of Teaching: The special meaning of the Tao Te Ching as related to the art and pleasures of teaching*. New York: D.I. Fine.

Scharf-Hunt, Diana, and Pam Hait. 1990. *The Tao of Time*. New York: Holt.

Watts, Alan. 1995. *The Tao of philosophy: The edited transcripts*. Boston: C.E. Tuttle.

Chapter 1. Introduction

Aldersey-Williams, Hugh, editor. 1990. *Cranbrook design: The new discourse*. New York: Rizzoli.

Alexander, Christopher. 1979. *The timeless way of building*. New York: Oxford University Press.

Bachelard, Gaston. 1994. *The poetics of space*. Translated by Maria Jolas. Boston: Beacon Press.

Blake, Peter. 1977. *Form follows fiasco: Why modern architecture hasn't worked*. Boston: Little, Brown.

Boudon, Philippe. 1972. *Lived-in architecture: Le Corbusier's Pessac revisited*. Translated by Gerald Onn. Cambridge, MA: MIT Press.

Brand, Stewart. 1994. *How buildings learn: What happens after they're built*. New York: Viking.

Branzi, Andrea. 1988. *Learning from Milan: Design and the second modernity.* Cambridge, MA: MIT Press.

Day, Christopher. 1995. *Places of the soul: Architecture and environmental design as a healing art.* London: Thorsons.

Duffy, Francis. 1992. *The changing workplace.* Edited by Patrick Hannay. London: Phaidon Press.

Holl, Steven. 1991. *Anchoring: Selected projects, 1975–1991,* 3rd edition. New York: Princeton Architectural Press.

Holl, Steven. 1996. *Intertwining: Selected projects 1989–1995.* New York: Princeton Architectural Press.

Jencks, Charles. 1991. *The language of post-modern architecture,* 6th edition. New York: Rizzoli.

Krohn, Lisa, and Michael McCoy. 1989. "Beyond beige: Interpretive design for the post-industrial age." *Design Issues* 5 (2) (Spring): 112–23.

Mackenzie, Dorothy. 1991. *Design for the environment.* New York: Rizzoli.

Mitchell, C. Thomas. 1993. Redefining designing: *From form to experience.* New York: Van Nostrand Reinhold.

Mitchell, C. Thomas. 1996. *New thinking in design: Conversations on theory and practice.* New York: Van Nostrand Reinhold.

Papanek, Victor J. 1995. *The green imperative: Natural design for the real world.* New York: Thames and Hudson.

"Peter Eisenman: An Architectural Design interview by Charles Jencks." 1988. *Architectural Design* 58 (3–4): 48–61.

Pevsner, Nikolaus. 1963. *An outline of European architecture,* 7th edition. Harmondsworth, England: Penguin Books.

Poynor, Rick. 1990. *Nigel Coates: The city in motion.* New York: Rizzoli.

Seamon, David, editor. 1993. *Dwelling, seeing, and designing: Toward a phenomenological ecology.* Albany, NY: State University of New York Press.

Seamon, David, and Robert Mugerauer, editors. 1985. *Dwelling, place, and environment: Towards a phenomenology of person and world.* New York: Columbia University Press.

Swafford, Jan. 1992. *The Vintage guide to classical music.* New York: Vintage Books.

Thackara, John, editor. 1988. *Design after modernism: Beyond the object.* New York: Thames and Hudson.

Venturi, Robert. 1966. *Complexity and contradiction in architecture.* New York: Museum of Modern Art.

Venturi, Robert, Denise Scott Brown, and Steven Izenour. 1972. *Learning from Las Vegas.* Cambridge, MA: MIT Press.

Wagner, Michael. 1993. "Creative catalyst." *Interiors* 152 (3) (March): 53–67.

Watts, Alan. 1995. *Become what you are.* Edited by Mark Watts. Boston: Shambhala.

Watts, Alan. 1995. *The Tao of philosophy: The edited transcripts.* Boston: C.E. Tuttle.

Watts, Alan. 1957. *The way of Zen.* New York: Pantheon.

Wolfe, Tom. 1981. *From Bauhaus to our house.* New York: Farrar, Straus, and Giroux.

Zaha M. Hadid. 1995. Edited and photographed by Yukio Futagawa; interview by Yoshio Futagawa. Tokyo: A.D.A. Edita.

Chapter 2. Daoist principles

Anthology of Chinese literature: From early times to the fourteenth century. 1965. Compiled and edited by Cyril Birch. New York: Grove Press.

Bloomfield, Frena. 1989. *The book of Chinese beliefs: A journey into the Chinese inner world.* New York: Ballantine Books.

Capra, Fritjof. 1975. *The Tao of physics: An exploration of the parallels between modern physics and Eastern mysticism.* Berkeley: Shambhala.

Chu Hsi. 1956. "Collected Works" in *Science and civilization in China, Vol. II.* Translated by Joseph Needham. Cambridge: Cambridge University Press.

Inn, Henry. 1950. *Chinese houses and gardens.* Edited by Shao Chang Lee. New York: Bonanza Books.

Jencks, Charles. 1985. *Modern movements in architecture,* 2nd edition. New York: Viking.

Jones, John Chris. 1991. *designing designing.* London: Architecture Design and Technology Press.

Lao-tsu. 1989. *The Tao Te Ching* [Yi Jing]. Translated by Ellen Chen. New York: Paragon House.

Lao Tzu [Laozi]. 1989. *Tao Teh Ching* [Dao De Jing]. Translated by John C. H. Wu. Boston: Shambhala.

Mitchell, C. Thomas. 1993. *Redefining designing: From form to experience.* New York: Van Nostrand Reinhold.

Peter, John. 1994. *The oral history of modern architecture: Interviews with the greatest architects of the twentieth century.* New York: Abrams.

Skinner, Stephen. 1982. *The living earth manual of Feng-Shui: Chinese geomancy.* London: Routledge and Kegan Paul.

The encyclopedia of Eastern philosophy and religion: Buddhism, Hinduism, Taoism, Zen. 1994. Boston: Shambhala.

The authentic I-Ching [Yi Jing]. 1987. Translated by Henry Wei. North Hollywood, CA: Newcastle Publishing.

Chapter 3. Feng Shui

Bloomfield, Frena. 1989. *The book of Chinese beliefs: A journey into the Chinese inner world.* New York: Ballantine Books.

Chatwin, Bruce. 1989. *What am I doing here?* New York: Viking.

Eitel, Ernest J. 1993. *Feng Shui,* with commentary by John Michell. Singapore: Graham Brash.

Glanzrock, Paul. 1995. "Banking on heritage at China Trust." *Facilities Design and Management* 14 (2) (February): 42–47.

Govert, Johndennis. 1993. *Feng Shui: Art and harmony of place.* Phoenix: Daikakuji Publications.

Gyatso, Geshe Kelsang. 1995. *The joyful path of good fortune: The complete guide to the Buddhist path to enlightenment,* 2nd revised edition. London: Tharpa Publications.

Kwok, Man-Ho, and Joanne O'Brien. 1991. *The elements of Feng Shui.* Shaftesbury, Dorset; Rockport, MA: Element.

Langdon, Philip. 1995. "Asia bound." *Progressive Architecture* 76 (3) (March): 43–51; 86, 88.

Lip, Evelyn. 1987. *Feng Shui: A layman's guide to Chinese geomancy.* Union City, CA: Heian International.

Lip, Evelyn. 1990. *Feng Shui for business.* Union City, CA: Heian International.

Lip, Evelyn. 1993. *Feng Shui for the home.* Union City, CA: Heian International.

O'Brien, Joanne, and Kwok Man Ho. 1991. *The elements of Feng Shui.* Rockport, MA: Element Books.

O'Neill, Molly. 1997. "Feng Shui or Feng Phooey?" *New York Times*, January 9: Sec. C, p. 1, col. 2.

Rossbach, Sarah. 1983. *Feng Shui: The Chinese art of placement.* New York: Dutton.

Rossbach, Sarah. 1991. *Interior design with Feng Shui.* New York: Arkana.

Rossbach, Sarah. 1994. *Living color: Master Lin Yun's guide to Feng Shui and the art of color.* New York: Kodansha International.

Skinner, Stephen. 1982. *The living earth manual of Feng-Shui: Chinese geomancy.* London: Routledge and Kegan Paul.

Sundstrom, Eric. 1986. *Work places: The psychology of the physical environment in offices and factories.* Cambridge; New York: Cambridge University Press.

Walters, Derek. 1991. *The Feng Shui handbook: A practical guide to Chinese geomancy.* London: Aquarian.

Waring, Philippa. 1993. *The way of Feng Shui: Harmony, health, wealth and happiness.* London: Souvenir Press.

Wong, Eva. 1996. *Feng-Shui: The ancient wisdom of harmonious living for modern times.* Boston: Shambhala.

Chapter 4. Dao in design

Chan, Wing-Tsit. 1950. "Man and nature in the Chinese garden" in *Chinese houses and gardens.* By Henry Inn, edited by Shao Chang Lee. New York: Bonanza Books.

Giles, Herbert Allen, editor. 1922. *Gems of Chinese literature.* Shanghai: Kelly and Walsh.

Keswick, Maggie. 1978. *The Chinese garden: History, art & architecture.* New York: Rizzoli.

Lie, Ji. 1968. *Yingzao fashi.* Taibei: Commercial Press.

Paludan, Ann. 1991. *The Chinese Spirit Road: The classical tradition of stone tomb statuary.* New Haven: Yale University Press.

Stein, Rolf A. 1987. *The world in miniature: Container gardens and dwellings in Far Eastern religious thought.* Translated by Phyllis Brooks. Stanford: Stanford University Press.

Tai Chen. 1968. *Kao kung chi tu.* Taibei: Commercial Press.

Chapter 5. Emerging trends in Western design

Aldersey-Williams, Hugh, editor. 1990. *Cranbrook design: The new discourse.* New York: Rizzoli.

Alexander, Christopher, et al. 1977. *A pattern language: Towns, buildings, construction.* New York: Oxford University Press.

Alexander, Christopher. 1979. *The timeless way of building.* New York: Oxford University Press.

Bachelard, Gaston. 1994. *The poetics of space.* Translated by Maria Jolas. Boston: Beacon Press.

Brand, Stewart. 1994. *How buildings learn: What happens after they're built.* New York: Viking.

Castelli, Clino Trini. "Design primario" in C. Thomas Mitchell. 1996. *New thinking in design: Conversations on theory and practice.* New York: Van Nostrand Reinhold: 62–71.

Coates, Nigel. "Street signs" in John Thackara, editor. 1988. *Design after modernism: Beyond the object.* New York: Thames and Hudson: 95–114.

"Contrasting concepts of harmony in architecture: Debate between Christopher Alexander and Peter Eisenman." 1983. *Lotus International* 40: 60–68.

Crosbie, Michael J. 1994. *Green architecture: A guide to sustainable design.* Rockport, MA: Rockport Publishers.

Day, Christopher. 1995. *Places of the soul: Architecture and environmental design as a healing art.* London: Thorsons.

Duffy, Francis. 1992. *The changing workplace,* edited by Patrick Hannay. London: Phaidon Press.

Duffy, Francis. "The choreography of change" in C. Thomas Mitchell. 1996. *New thinking in design: Conversations on theory and practice.* New York: Van Nostrand Reinhold: 26 - 39.

Eno, Brian. 1996. *A year with swollen appendices.* London; Boston: Faber and Faber.

Farmer, John. 1996. *Green shift: Towards a green sensibility in architecture.* Oxford: Butterworth-Heinemann.

Halprin, Lawrence. 1969. *The RSVP cycles: Creative processes in the human environment.* New York: Braziller.

Hans Hollein, design: Man transforms. 1989. Vienna: Locker.

Hughes, Robert. 1991. *Shock of the new,* revised edition. New York: Knopf.

Jencks, Charles. 1993. *Architecture today,* 2nd edition. London: Academy Editions.

Jencks, Charles. 1991. *The language of post-modern architecture,* 6th edition. New York: Rizzoli.

Jencks, Charles. 1985. *Towards a symbolic architecture: The thematic house.* New York: Rizzoli.

Krohn, Lisa, and Michael McCoy. 1989. "Beyond beige: Interpretive design for the post-industrial age." *Design Issues* 5 (2) (Spring): 112–123.

Kroll, Lucien. "Contemporaneous architecture" in C. Thomas Mitchell. 1996. *New thinking in design: Conversations on theory and practice.* New York: Van Nostrand Reinhold: 42–60.

Lopez Barnett, Dianna, and William D. Browning. 1995. *A primer on sustainable building.* Snowmass, CO: Rocky Mountain Institute.

Mackenzie, Dorothy. 1991. *Design for the environment.* New York: Rizzoli.

McCoy, Michael. "Interpretive design" in C. Thomas Mitchell. 1996. *New thinking in design: Conversations on theory and practice.* New York: Van Nostrand Reinhold: 2–11.

McDonough, William. 1993. "Design, ecology, ethics and the making of things: A centennial sermon," February 7 (unpublished typescript).

McDonough, William. 1993. "The Hannover Principles." Reprinted in *Interiors* 152 (3) (March): 52.

Mitchell, C. Thomas. 1993. *Redefining designing: From form to experience.* New York: Van Nostrand Reinhold.

Moughtin, Cliff. 1996. *Urban design: Green dimensions.* Oxford: Butterworth-Heinemann.

Papanek, Victor J. 1995. *The green imperative: Natural design for the real world.* New York: Thames and Hudson.

Pettena, Gianni. 1988. *Hans Hollein: Works, 1960–1988.* Milano; New York: Idea Books.

Poynor, Rick. 1990. *Nigel Coates: The city in motion.* New York: Rizzoli.

Rasmussen, Steen Eiler. 1962. *Experiencing architecture,* 2nd U.S. edition. Translated by Eve Wendt. Cambridge, MA: MIT Press.

Rheinfrank, John. From an unpublished interview with C. Thomas Mitchell, 1991.

Schlossberg, Edwin. "Creating conversations" in C. Thomas Mitchell. 1996. *New thinking in design: Conversations on theory and practice.* New York: Van Nostrand Reinhold: 72–79.

Schwartz, Peter. 1991. *The art of the long view: Planning for the future in an uncertain world.* New York: Doubleday Currency.

Schwartz, Peter. "Scenario planning" in C. Thomas Mitchell. 1996. *New thinking in design: Conversations on theory and practice.* New York: Van Nostrand Reinhold: 139 - 148.

Seamon, David, editor. 1993. *Dwelling, seeing, and designing: Toward a phenomenological ecology.* Albany, NY: State University of New York Press.

Seamon, David, and Robert Mugerauer, editors. 1985. *Dwelling, place and environment: Towards a phenomenology of person and world.* New York: Columbia University Press.

SITE. 1989. New York: Rizzoli.

Tschumi, Bernard. 1994. *Architecture and disjunction.* Cambridge, MA: MIT Press.

Tschumi, Bernard. 1994. *Event-cities: Praxis.* Cambridge, MA: MIT Press.

Tschumi, Bernard. 1994. *The Manhattan transcripts,* 2nd edition. London: Academy Editions.

U.S. Congress. Office of Technology Assessment. 1992. *Green products by design: Choices for a cleaner environment.* Washington, DC: GPO.

Vale, Brenda, and Robert Vale. 1991. *Green architecture: Design for an energy-conscious future.* Boston: Little, Brown.

Venturi, Robert. 1966. *Complexity and contradiction in architecture.* New York: Museum of Modern Art, 1966.

Venturi, Robert, Denise Scott Brown, and Steven Izenour. 1972. *Learning from Las Vegas.* Cambridge, MA: MIT Press.

Wagner, Michael. 1993. "Creative catalyst." *Interiors* 152 (3) (March): 53–67.

Wines, James. 1991. "Inside outside: The aesthetic implications of green design." *Interior Design* 62 (11) (August): 114–119.

Wines, James. 1987. *De-architecture.* New York: Rizzoli.

Chapter 6. Conclusion

Jones, John Chris. 1991. *designing designing*. London: Architecture Design and Technology Press.

Index

About the Authors

C. Thomas Mitchell is a tenured professor in the interior design program at Indiana University, Bloomington, and director of the Center for Design Process, a research lab exploring innovative, user-responsive approaches to design. In the forefront of design thinking, he is the author of *Redefining Designing* and *New Thinking in Design*.

Jiangmei Wu is a computer graphics artist and multimedia developer at Hirons & Company. She holds a B.A. degree in architecture from Tongi University in China and an M.A. degree in interior design from Indiana University.